CAUSLEY AT 70

Hastings-on-Hudson, New York, 1984. Photo by Christopher P. Stephens

Causley At 70

edited by Harry Chambers

PETERLOO POETS

First published in 1987
by Peterloo Poets
2 Kelly Gardens . Calstock . Cornwall PL18 9SA
Printed in Great Britain by
Latimer Trend & Company Ltd Plymouth

ISBN 0–905291–89–1

ACKNOWLEDGEMENTS

Grateful acknowledgement is made to Macmillan for permission to reprint the poems 'Walking', 'Timothy Winters' and 'Immunity' by Charles Causley, all from *Collected Poems*.

Grateful acknowledgement is made to The Celandine Press for permission to reprint 'Boulge', 'Bridie Wiles' and 'In The Dome Car' from *Twenty-one Poems* by Charles Causley (The Celandine Press, 1986).

Grateful acknowledgement is made to the University of Exeter Library for supplying photographs of the worksheets for 'Immunity' from a notebook in the Causley archive.

'A Kitchen In The Morning' by Charles Causley was first published in *Poetry Review* June 1982.

'So Slowly To Harbour' by Charles Causley was first published in the *The Listener*, 17 March 1977.

Grateful acknowledgement is made to The Estate of Philip Larkin for permission to reprint the poem by Philip Larkin beginning 'Dear CHARLES . . .' ('A Birthday Card'). Previously untitled, this first appeared in *Poems For Charles Causley* edited by Michael Hanke (The Enitharmon Press, 1982), a volume which marked the poet's 65th birthday.

'Causley's Ballads' by Stanley Cook is an extract from an article that first appeared in *The School Librarian*, December 1976.

'As New As It Is Old' by Ronald Tamplin was first published in *New Poetry* (ed. Norman Hidden), 1979.

'The Poetry of Charles Causley' by Edward Levy was first published in *P. N. Review* 6, 1977.

'Farewell, for Charles Causley' by Colin MacInnes is an extract from his book *England, Half English* (MacGibbon & Kee, 1961 & Penguin Books, 1966.)

The photograph of 'Camels and the Solar Telephone at William Creek S. A.' that illustrates Fay Zwicky's poem 'The Call' is by courtesy of *The Age*, Melbourne.

Grateful acknowledgement is made to Ralph Steadman for permission to reproduce his cover drawing (page 73) from *Timothy Winters* (No. 7 in the series Contemporary Poetry set to Music), Turret Books, 1970.

The photographs on pages 54 and 112 are from productions of Dylan Thomas's *The Doctor and the Devils* adapted for The Music Theatre Studio Ensemble by Charles Causley with music by Stephen McNeff and performed at The Banff Centre School of Fine Arts, Alberta, Canada in March 1984. (Courtesy of George Ross, Manager, Theatre Arts, The Banff School of Fine Arts.)

The photographs on page 2 (opposite full title page) and page 35 are by Christopher P. Stephens.

The photograph on page 6 (opposite Contents page) is by Christopher Barker.

The photographs on pages 37 and 105 are by Mark Gerson.

The photograph on page 111 is by Carol Hughes.

Cover illustration: Portrait Drawing of Charles Causley by Robert Tilling R. I.

At his home in Launceston, 1986. Photo by Christopher Barker

CONTENTS

POEM & PROSE TRIBUTES

BY CHARLES CAUSLEY

A GREETINGS CARD FOR CHARLES CAUSLEY ON HIS SEVENTIETH BIRTHDAY

Roger Pringle

Clear as the water drawn from Cyprus Well,
Hewn like the slates that roof your granite home,
Anchored to cheer despite death's drenching swell,
Rooted in Cornwall's soil and Eden's loam;
Let all who've known your art of three decades
Enhance their sense of life, both old and young,
Send greetings cards (by way of accolades),

Calling to mind some themes that you have sung:
Angels and aunts, Australia's heat and dust,
Union Street pussers, ugly scenes of war,
Stories of saints and ghosts, betrayals of trust,
Lovers and loners, songs of sea and shore.
Enthralled and greedy, one thing more we ask:
Your gifts keep coming—just a birthday task!

FAITHFUL TRAVELLING

D. M. Thomas

Reading 'Gudow' in Charles's latest collection, *Secret Destinations*, I remembered sharply the shared experience which inspired the poem. We were on a British Council tour in West Germany; we both wanted to see the border; a young German writer drove us from Hamburg to a desolate spot where East and West confronted each other across barbed wire. The eeriness moved us, and it was predictable that we would both try to capture it in verse. My poem was a general atmospheric impression; Charles's was packed with observed details: 'The road frays to a halt. A dyke/Of little frogs and Indian ink/Right-angles it. A ladder pinked/Half-wasting to a tree swings like/The hanged man. Restless, overhead,/A bird-hide drifts apart . . .'

From his description I remembered it all, yet I hadn't noticed it at the time. 'My God!' I thought. 'Why didn't *I* see it?' The three of us had stood quietly for a few minutes, observing, reflecting; Charles had not whipped-out a notebook and biro, nor clicked a camera; yet it seemed, on my reading his poem, as if his eye or his mind were fitted with some ultra-sensitive technology, which enabled him to record unerringly; at the same time to find the simple unerring metaphor. The road did 'fray' to a halt. Precisely.

Economy is one of the most striking features of his style. Every adjective, every verb, conveys a complexity of emotion, and no word is ever used just for the sake of the metre or rhyme. The same economy is displayed in his character. I had a taste of this on the day following our drive to Gudow. The British Council had planned our itinerary from an out-of-date plane-timetable; at Hamburg airport we found we had missed our flight to Düsseldorf. I panicked: we would miss our evening engagement.

Charles was unperturbed. 'Are the guns firing, Don?' he asked.

Momentarily taken aback, I chuckled: 'No!'

'Well, then, it's alright. If the guns aren't firing, it's alright.'

For him, of course, the guns had fired, during his years as a matelot. It put a missed plane into perspective. He will go to

10

endless trouble to help a person in distress; but if a German audience waited in vain for us—so what? It wasn't our fault. Perhaps 'Gudow' was developing in his imagination. We made our Düsseldorf engagement.

He is one of our finest poets because his imagination is both immensely sophisticated and childlike: childlike in its wonderment and generosity. Every time we meet, he bubbles over with praise for a book he has been reading. 'Have you read—?' he asks. 'It's jolly good! *Jolly* good!' Leaving him, I rush to the nearest bookshop.

I feel annoyed when some ignorant reviewer summarises him as the finest living writer of ballads. Of course it's true; but much more of his beautiful talent has gone into the lyrics, which— especially over the last decade—have become more disturbing and more profound. The surface simplicity of his style is deceptive. Many poets are simple, while appearing to be profound; Causley, like Frost, is the opposite.

I was once introducing him to a student-group at an Arvon Course in Devon, and for the first and only time in my life I completely dried. I became literally dumb. What was in my mind was the huge distance he had travelled from the struggling, working-class home in Launceston, between the wars. His vision encompassed the world, and the world of art; yet he had remained faithful to his origins, his voice still held the tones of moorland granite, the sea, and soft Tamar-side valleys. I glimpsed the effort, the courage, behind all his faithful travelling. Who could tell that from his laconic, friendly manner, that humorous, throwaway Cornish speech? The thought moved me deeply—and that's why I lost my tongue.

BIRTHDAY GREETINGS

Ted Hughes

I meant to rhyme your dream:
All Cornwall
A willawaw sea
Of Moors and Mounts
Bursting to granite foam,
A tide-rip cemetery---
One erupting tomb
Of oracular Menhir bones
Which called each other by name
To limber up their tons
Dancing in circles
Backs to the centre backwards
To undo time

But you were polishing a find.
You were rehearsing
The perfect pitch
Of a granny's retort
To the postman's laugh
That morning in Launceston.

I had meant to paint
With Turneresque tints
Your spectacles' reflection
Of a storm-haven---
Boscastle to Penzance---
And anchored there
In the gold roads of evening,
Above those bleak, wet chapels,
On cabbage-leaf and quernstone
Cornwall's fleet of saints

But you were bent
At Altarnun
To a gravestone relief
Cut with a nail---
And the heart-broken sculptor,
His fame abandoned,
Curled in straw.

I had found an image:
You lie in the Irish Sea.
Like any son
Fallen from heaven
Across his mother's knee.
The Moon keeps the tides
Working the mines
That centuries of tinners
Deepened in your sides---
And whispering up your veins
Every one of the waves
Is a rough old Cornishman
Telling of his lives

But you were at thirty thousand feet
Entering Canadian air-space or were just
Touching down on the tarmac home
From home in Sydney.

No matter where. Cornwall
Is in you the same
As in Camel River
That stone with the name

Of the King who fell there
Under the overhang,
Is the freed water's
Threshold and tongue.

Congratulations, Charles.
God give us half the wit
To recognise our own
And to stick with it.

MAN OF THE WORLD

J. C. Trewin

A couple of years after the war, when I was editing (from London) *The West Country Magazine*, a poem arrived, in immaculate typescript, from Launceston. It was much the most exciting I had received. Others followed it. Today I prize the bound volumes of the magazine (which lasted for six years) for those early numbers and the birth, in effect, of a great poet. Though I have always been dubious about using the major epithets—'Think how they'll look in the future!' my first editor used to say—I have never been doubtful for a moment of applying them to Charles Causley. A very early poem was 'Keats at Teignmouth: Spring 1818'; I was happy to see it, years ahead, as the first in Charles's collected edition, with its unforgettable stanzas (listen to the vowels):

> When spring fired her fusilladoes
>   Salt spray, sea-spray on the sill,
> When the budding scarf of April
>   Ravelled on the Devon hill,
>
> Then I saw the crystal poet
>   Leaning on the old sea-rail;
> In his breast lay death, the lover,
>   In his head, the nightingale.

There was so much else: 'The Seasons in North Cornwall':

> My room is a bright glass cabin,
>   All Cornwall thunders at my door,
> And the white ships of winter lie
>   In the sea-roads of the moor;

'Legend' (with Winter that 'lay, like Gulliver,/ Over the tiny town'; and 'At Porth Veor' ('The sea pulling over the pebbles/ With long salt fingers below me').

Around this time, too, when I was literary editor of *The Observer*, a poem called 'King's College Chapel', in the same perfect typescript, arrived from Launceston by the morning post:

When to the music of Byrd or Tallis,
　The ruffed boys singing in the blackened stalls,
The candles lighting the small bones on their faces,
　The Tudors stiff in marble on the walls. . .

I ran down, not bothering to take the lift, to the Editor, Ivor Brown. Biting his handkerchief as usual, he was sitting glumly with his secretary and a pile of letters in which he seemed deeply uninterested. (Political, probably). Two or three times he read the script I handed to him before he looked up. 'Yes,' he said. 'That's a *poem!*' Anyone who knew the notoriously monosyllabic I.B. in those days would have realised that the four words and the implied exclamation mark were equivalent to a knighthood.

With the years Charles Causley became one of the most admired poets of his period: admired for his command of mood; his unfaltering sense of place; the surprises in line upon line; the compassion; the humour; the generosity, as in his admiration for the blind and deaf Jack Clemo, poet of the Cornish clay-lands; his knowledge of children ('Timothy Winters'); the technical assurance, by no means in ballad-quality alone; and his way of carrying one to the empyrean with a single phrase. Though I had never been a hoarder, I have collected (thanks to him) his books and his letters.

Two incidents linger. One was in about 1961. We—my wife Wendy, our two sons, and myself—were sitting at dinner during the ebb of a summer evening in the courtyard of a very quiet *pensione* off the Piazza de Comune in Assisi. Suddenly we heard a tapping on the glass door and Wendy's name called through the Umbrian twilight. Astonished, we looked round. This was our first visit to Italy; we had not expected to see anybody from home, certainly not from Cornwall. But there, outside, was Charles Causley with a former naval friend: it reminded me for a moment of an old Cornish neighbour at The Lizard, very long before, who had said, when her son went to London: 'You'll meet him going down street.' (There, alas, nothing happened).

To see Charles was a joy. He and his friend, an art teacher, had come up from Rome. It was the beginning of a splendid brevity during which I remember a great deal of laughter, inseparable from Charles, and an afternoon when we took a car to the Eremo delle Carceri—the Franciscan retreat in the hills where we saw, in

15

a grotto, the hollowed stone upon which Francis had slept. A wholly delightful priest objected ·to Wendy's sleeveless dress and lent her a scarf to cover her upper arms. We still have on our mantelpiece a colour-photograph of us all, with the priest, Charles, Wendy (sinful dress without scarf), and our sons, Ion, then eighteen, and Mark, who was eleven.

Some time after this, during the Edinburgh Festival of 1965, Charles shared an evening's poetry reading at the Freemasons' Hall in George Street, a lesson, I thought, to his colleagues (Auden was one): not a hint of an exhibition or a tedious duty, but the warm tones showing in every curl of rhythm, every inflection, why the work had been written; the creative mind behind the creative voice.

By now, I suppose, I must have read all Charles's work, including the early prose stories, *Hands to Dance and Skylark*, which no collector should miss: we had two in *West Country*. To find an epigraph for the poet I would go straight to a line from 'Legend', nearly four decades ago: 'Set forth so, imagination!' His own imagination has been uncanny, always with the words to match it: knowledge that, for me, glorified those editorial days far back, the newspaper office in Tudor Street, the fleeting stay in Umbria, the Edinburgh night.

He has long been, of course, the laureate of his own Cornwall: the 'True Ballad of Sir Henry Trecarell' (who rebuilt the Launceston parish church of St Mary Magdalene); 'What do I remember of my home town?'; 'The Ballad of Charlotte Dymond'; 'Mary, Mary, Magdalene/Lying on the wall'; and the 'Short Life of Nevil Northey Burnard', sculptor, with its superb opening:

> Here lived Burnard who with his finger's bone
> Broke syllables of light from the moorstone,
> Spat on the genesis of dust and clay,
> Rubbed with sure hands the blinded eyes of day,
> And through the seasons of the talking sun
> Walked, calm as God, the fields of Altarnun.

And Cornwall is in 'Innocent's Song' ('Who's that knocking on the window?... Why do his yellow, yearning eyes/Burn like saffron buns?'), the poem that ends with the terrifying lines:

16

Watch where he comes walking
Out of the Christmas flame,
Dancing, double-talking:

Herod is his name.

Very well; but today of many happy returns he is a national,
international poet, a poet of the world, evoking (as in the
collection, *Secret Destinations*) Canada, Australia, the places where
he has written and taught and laughed. He is a Queen's Gold
Medallist. He holds the CBE and a doctorate (of Exeter). And he
is always Charles Causley of Launceston: the Cornishman who, in
the splendour of his mind and the generosity of his spirit, has
never failed to summon to him every responsive imagination.

*With Samuel Menashe and an unidentified member of the audience after a reading at Frank Scioscia's
Bookstore, Hastings-on-Hudson, New York, 1984.*

THE CALL

(for Charles Causley)

Fay Zwicky

hello Charles how are ya
mate remember William
Creek I can't talk
long there's other fellers
waiting and a string of
camels kneeling on the edge
of nowhere and a bloody
great phone box stuck in
the sand like a dunny with
everyone wanting to use
it no poetry's nothing like
life not mine anyway if what
I think a poem is a poem
poets are born not made just
like you said but life does
help eh tell them all to drop
dead I'm talking to a poet
yes it's Australia saltbush
sand and spinifex and 45°
in the shade last week not
Cornwall in the winter eh
the South Australian manager
of Telecom told us it will
change our lives a facility
he called it for what that's
worth Bernie's cranky it's not
hotter they'll do just about
anything for a dogfight here
gets chilly on the Simpson
three dogs and a road train
full of horses for the knackers
in Whyalla and a bunch of
paper men photographers the
blokes who put it in and
tourists looking zonked the
manager unveiled the bloody
thing usually only 6 of us not
much to see and less to do
bit of a treat really otherwise
we wouldn't get to see each other
all that often spotted nearly
60 all in all here today and

18

gone tomorrow plus the manager
that young stuffed shirt a
trendy wouldn't touch the amber
fluid wanted wine facility this
facility that me camel's got his
nose in piss off you whiffy bastard
not you old mate I'll write a
proper letter later none of
this microwave stuff with
pips to stop congratulations
anyway there's a strangler in
a cowboy suit bashing down the
door and me camel's dropped
his bundle see ya

Camels and the Solar Telephone at William Creek S. A. (Courtesy of *The Age*, Melbourne)

FOR CHARLES CAUSLEY

(on his 70th Birthday)

Elizabeth Jennings

Cornwall is your pasture and your pleasure,
The granite cliffs, the high sea, and each cove
The sea rides into puts us at our leisure

For we are tourists. We know little of
The spell of that long sweep of England where
You've lived so long that Cornwall is a love

You'll never lose. In bracing, salty air,
In high white horses all the year round, you
Have now become a part of all that's there.

The open and the secret places know
Your step and gaze. So now I praise a place
And doing so I offer thanks to you

For all your poetry and its lyric grace
Which are so rare now. You have taught me much
About the need to work upon my verse.

I see you seldom yet I feel in touch.

CHARLES CAUSLEY

Norman Levine

In February 1954 Charles Causley accepted a poem of mine called 'Crabbing' that he used on *Apollo in the West*, a BBC, West Region, literary programme that he was editing. And that began a correspondence that developed into a friendship that has gone on since.

I was living (not long) in St Ives, not long married, and my friends were the painters near my age. These days people look back to the 1950's in St Ives as one of the peaks of creative work being done anywhere. Ben Nicholson, Barbara Hepworth, Bernard Leach, were the older generation. And Peter Lanyon, Patrick Heron, Terry Frost, Bryan Wynter, were among the younger. In fact, from the young painters, it was only Peter Lanyon who was there then. The others were all up-country teaching or living, for a while, elsewhere.

I began to exchange letters with Charles in Launceston. And began to talk about him to Peter in St Ives. It seemed the most logical thing for me to arrange for them to meet. It was a bleak winter day, no snow, but damp when Peter drove me in his van to the Jamaica Inn on the edge of Bodmin Moor. Charles was to come from Launceston, across the Moor, and meet us there.

They had something in common. Two young (and proud to be) Cornishmen. Both had served in the Armed Forces away from England. Charles on a destroyer and Peter in the RAF, in the Middle East and Italy, as a fitter.

Perhaps it was because we were in the War and, after it was over, wanted to do something in painting or writing, that brought us together. Or, perhaps, because in those days writers and painters tended to seek each other's company. We had the energy, the enthusiasm, and the optimism, of all beginners. Peter had his first exhibition in London. Charles had two small books of poems published by Erica Marx at The Hand and Flower Press. I had a slim book of verse and a novel I wanted to forget. And though these first steps had been taken we were, in 1954, quite unknown.

So there we were in Jamaica Inn. The only customers on a cold winter evening. The proprietor, behind the bar, had a blazing fire going all evening in the large fireplace. We drank. We ate. We talked. I can't remember what we talked about. But, right from the start, the proprietor refused to take any money. We assumed this was very civilised behaviour and we would settle what we drank and ate when we left.

Several hours later when we decided to leave, to drive back where we lived, the three of us went to the bar to settle the bill. He still refused to take any money. We wondered why.

'When you are next on the BBC ... if you could mention Jamaica Inn ...'

Outside, in the dark, we laughed. And decided it was a case of mistaken identity. He obviously thought we were someone else. Part of some BBC programme like *Down Your Way* ...

From the beginning I found that Charles's notion of being a friend was to encourage you to be a writer. And he worked at this friendship. He sent people to see me. He reviewed a new book when it appeared. He arranged for radio and TV programmes to happen. He put things my way ... He also wrote me letters and postcards.

What he did with these letters and postcards was to keep reminding me that I was a writer. The encouragement came not so much from what he said but from what he took for granted. And I don't expect I was the only one that he did this to.

I have been re-reading them recently. They not only give a picture of those early days but they, inevitably, connect with his work. A postcard, black and white, from Launceston of St Stephen's Church:

St Stephen's Church School: just
along the road is where my mother
saw the dancing bear.

His letters and cards would tell me what he was doing, where he had things out, of books that he read that he thought I might like. And, in the immediate post-war years when there were mostly amateurs about, he gave a sense of being professional:

Am bashing on with new poems: just finished a group of six. Can you tell me of any Canadian or American magazines that pay? I'm all for this if possible.

He tried to do this not only with his own work but also with the work of his friends. One time it was for Jack Clemo:

If you think any Canadian magazine
may be interested in any of Jack's poems . . .

A few years later he wrote the same thing for some poems of D. M. Thomas.

I began to go and see him in Launceston. 'Take the early bus, its quicker and cheaper, and you can spend the day here.' And he would meet me at the bus-stop (he was always dependable) . . . show me the sights and how places connected with the past . . . take me out to a good meal . . . go to a good pub . . . show me the places that appeared in his work. But what impressed me most was the way he was saying Hello, right and left, as we walked through the streets. Everyone seemed to know him . . . young men and women, girls and boys . . . people he had taught as a schoolmaster . . . their parents. I envied him this. He belonged to the place where he lived. In St Ives most of the artists I knew (apart from Peter Lanyon) had come from somewhere else.

And then he began to come and visit us in St Ives. As a teacher and deputy headmaster it was usually only at half-term that he could do this:

Hope to be down on Sunday. Could we meet around opening time in one of the pubs—say—on the harbour? We'll keep an eye open for you: please arr: red carpet, band, local celebrities etc . . .

He was interested in the West Penwith . . . in the painters I knew, as well as the literary figures (from the past: Katherine Mansfield, D. H. Lawrence) where they lived. Perhaps what, also, drew us together was the Canadian connection. I had left Canada, in 1949, to come to England because I wanted to be a writer:

I forgot if I ever told you but my father was born in Canada and was christened in Trinity Church, St Thomas, Ontario. Immigrant parents: they returned to Devon just before the first World War. And my mother's brother also emigrated before the first War, worked as a lumberjack, joined up over there, died as a young soldier of pneumonia, and is buried in some military cemetery there somewhere (I think Quebec). Anyhow the facts are around the house somewhere. I was

23

named (middle name) after him: and in my own personal mythology he's a figure rather like Rowse's Uncle Cheelie, who emigrated to S. Africa in *Cornish Childhood*. Do you know this?

But those early years, despite the difficulties, always evoked from Charles: a sympathetic response, the need to get on with the work, and a sense of enjoyment and fun. In a postcard to my wife he wrote:

I've been yelling with laughter at Norman sending my name to that Belgian *Who's Who*, because I sent his. They probably think we're Siamese Twins.

And one to me:

Spent a hilarious evening with Laurie Lee. We played and sang folk-songs nonstop, real and faked. (As oi went out wan morning/ on the 65th of Juin).

The letters, the postcards, kept coming. Something in Charles has made him a world traveller. (Was it the War that did that as well?) I used to ask him, in those early years, would he leave Launceston? He always said, perhaps. Why not? He has, in fact, left it often. He is the most travelled person I know. But he comes back.

He may sometimes appear to be distant. As if he is playing his cards close to his chest. But he warms up quickly. And always the instinct for connections. When our eldest daughter left St Ives to go to Manchester university he wrote to my wife:

I love Manchester: a beautiful & romantic place in my day (1943/44) & the people even better. I found myself as a poet here. Be warned.

(And signed himself) J. Tar.

He may be amused to be reminded in this his 70th year that he once wrote, on another postcard, in 1958:

I've done poems for various books—one for the Eliot—70th—birthday one.

Perhaps this need, of making connections, came from realizing

24

he was the last of the Causleys. Once we had arranged to meet in Plymouth, in a bookshop, he told me he had come, not long, from burying his last maiden Aunt in Trusham, in Devon. And I remember that marvellous poem, 'Walking':

Walking the lane's long-grave, the day
Fresh-dug with flowers and grasses thick
I felt the air with may turn sick,
And at the scent, and at the sound
Of water fighting from the ground,
Time and the hour thinned away.

You stood there: the same crackling dress
And that antique, huge-buttoned coat,
Brooch clear as coal pinned at your throat,
The lively hair caught in a bun,
Your face pecked by the clucking sun,
The voice as cool as watercress.

Straw hat, umbrella sleek and spread;
But neither one of these could hold
The storm that broke inside your head
Or keep you from the final cold.
And now the earth is on your face
And I am in another place.

Here, children by an altered moor
Stamp suds of may on a green floor
As under waving skies a trawl
Of hawthorn drags the orchard wall.
Slowly the sun winks a gilt eye.
Birds, dark as history, lumber by.

The poems (I have my favourites) I remember without having to memorize them. And when I am away, living as now, in Toronto ... with the small paintings by Peter Lanyon, Bryan Wynter, Terry Frost, near ... and from the back window—so much green—watch a pair of cardinals as they try to get their only surviving youngster to fly from the vine (where they built the nest) to the nearest tree I suddenly, for no apparent reason, think of Cornwall. And it is to Charles' books that I go and re-read. And they bring back the people, the places, and those years.

THE DWINDLING ONES

(for Charles Causley)

John Heath-Stubbs

Upon your Cornish moors, I've read somewhere
There dwells a race of beings, para-human,
Who, for some ill they did, curse they incurred,
Are doomed continually to dwindle. Once they were giants,
Looming out of the mist, bawling into the storm-wind,
And then of super-human stature, great pine trunks their
    spears,
Hurling huge rocks for chuck-stones,
After human sized; then more and more dwarfish—
Mannikins, midgets, elvish urchins,
Piskyish carousers out of acorn-cups,
Bee-sucking cowslip-lurkers like Ariel;
Then miniscule, like tiny bugs
(Their war with the pismires is an epic theme)
Or gossamer-drifting money-spiders,
Exiguous as fleas, as thrips, as cheese-mites;
And then dimension of the animalculae—
Housed on the paramaecium, the rotifer a Charybdis,
Until at length they pass, with the viruses,
Through the fine filter of an eggshell porcelain.

The end of the ages will be their vanishing-point:
At Gabriel's trump they'll disappear,
With an imperceptible puff, a supersonic twang.
They have all time, but no eternity.

But you and I, Charles, at three-score and ten,
Must learn we live on Chronos his overdraft.
We'll laugh and lie down, we'll go to bed with our boots on,
And thank God for His bounty of mortality.

A DREAM OF LAUNCESTON

(for Charles Causley)

Alan Brownjohn

So clear and safe and small,
on the nearest horn of
about twenty-seven

steady-breathing fellows
who keep me cornered in
a field in North Cornwall

with their overbearing
friendliness (is it that?),
the ladybird allows

a petticoat of wing
and then recovers it.
And then: one pink-and-blue

nose lifts, and a deep note
rides out over the grass
to tremble the yellows

of the low primroses. . .
And 'Shoo!' I say, and 'Shoo!'
in my nine year-old voice

each time the dream comes back.
They do not shoo, and I
will not grow up, at all.

I read the numbers on
the twitching ears as if
nothing more happened next;

and crave the freedom of
that tiny elegance
To flaunt itself, and fly.

THE INDEPENDENCE OF CHARLES CAUSLEY

Dana Gioia

Charles Causley has stood apart from the mainstream of contemporary poetry. His work bears little relation to the most celebrated achievements of the modernist movement but refers back to older, more specifically English roots. Taking his inspiration from popular folk song and ballad, Causley stands with writers, such as A.E. Houseman, Thomas Hardy, Rudyard Kipling, Walter de la Mare, Robert Graves, John Betjeman, and perhaps Philip Larkin, who are part of a conservative counter-tradition in English letters which stresses the fundamentally national nature of its poetry and the critical role of popular forms in its inspiration.

Much of Causley's poetry has been written in the ballad form. Indeed he is the most celebrated and accomplished living writer of ballads in English, but his achievements are not so narrowly focused as many critics believe. He has mastered an impressive variety of forms, and the true unity of his work is not found so much in any specific allegiance to a particular form like the ballad but rather in his commitment to certain traditional virtues of English poetry—simplicity, clarity, grace, and compassion. He holds the steadfast conviction that the popular forms of English poetry are living modes of expression, despite the modernist revolution, choosing to write in simple, traditional forms in a period which prizes originality and complexity. He has endorsed the importance of narrative verse in an age which has called the very notion of poetic narrative into question. This conservatism has placed Causley in a radically independent position among contemporary poets, but ultimately he is less important for his independent stance than for the excellence and integrity of his verse. He is a potent reminder that talent often travels on a path divergent from the age.

In 1951 Causley brought out his first collection, *Farewell, Aggie Weston*, a small pamphlet of thirty-one poems. The distillation of Causley's six years in the navy, these poems vividly recreate the alternatingly intoxicating and sobering experiences of a generation of young Englishmen who in fighting World War II discovered the wider world. Most of the poems depict the sailor's life in wartime, both on ship and in the strange port cities he visits on leave. In its colorful portrayal of navy life *Farwell, Aggie Weston* remains one of the most representative books of English poetry to emerge from World War II, and the poem 'Chief Petty Officer' has become a definitive poem of the period capturing a kind of naval character who typified, for better or worse, the British military traditions that won the war. The book also has documentary importance since the poems incorporate a wealth of traditional and contemporary naval slang (much of which the author explains in footnotes). Like Kipling fifty years before him, Causley believed that the only way he could truly capture the unique character of a group of men was to use their special language, and in so doing he provided an interesting record of a particular time and place.

Although *Farewell, Aggie Weston* is not Causley's best book, it already shows him as an accomplished poet with a distinctive voice and perspective. It also foreshadows both the themes and techniques of his later work. The book contains poems written in both free and formal verse, and Causley uses both techniques in idiosyncratic ways to which he will return repeatedly in his subsequent career. His free verse is loose, cadenced speech used mainly for carefully detailed descriptive poems, whereas his metered poems, which are cast mainly in rhymed quatrains, especially various ballad stanzas, are used mostly for narrative and dramatic poems. Not surprisingly, given Causley's later eminence as a master of traditional forms, the best poems in *Farewell, Aggie Weston* are in thyme and meter, usually cast as ballads, such as his memorable 'Nursery Rhyme of Innocence and Experience'.

Although Causley's second volume, *Survivor's Leave* (1953), does not mark a broadening of his poetic concerns, it demonstrates a liberating concentration. Abandoning cadenced free verse and the aesthetic of raw experience it embodies, Causley perfected the tightly formal poems for which he would become best known. All of the poems in *Survivor's Leave* are written in rhyme and meter, a common coin which he now uses in a distinctively personal way. His rhythms move with deliberate regularity, and the diction has a timeless traditional quality. Full rhymes ring loudly at the end of each line. Sometimes unsophisticated to the point of crudity, this verse often has the texture of folk poetry or popular song, which gives it an unusual openness and immediacy. In an age when most poets writing in rhyme and meter try to disguise or underplay the formal patterns of their verse, Causley is a radical traditionalist, a primitive, who is unabashedly direct with his forms in a way unmatched by any contemporary poet except John Betjeman.

Survivor's Leave also demonstrates Causley's growing mastery of the ballad and contains two of his finest poems in that form, 'Recruiting Drive' and 'Ballad of the Faithless Wife'. In these and other poems one notices the influence of Auden's work, which provided Causley with a model of how to rejuvenate this traditional form with bold metaphors and the use of archetypal figures. But while Causley learned much from Auden, his work is never derivative. Causley's well-known poem 'On Seeing a Poet of the First World War at the Station of Abbeville' (a composite portrait based on Edmund Blunden, Siegfried Sassoon, and the poet's father), for example, incorporates techniques from Auden's lyrics but Causley uses them to achieve effects that are particularly his own.

As his title suggests, Causley's major theme in *Survivor's Leave* is once again war, though here the conflict has been universalized beyond World War II in a tragic view of life as a doomed struggle between the evil and the innocent. The book is permeated with images of violence and deception. In 'Recruiting Drive', a butcher bird lures young men to their deaths in battle. In 'Cowboy Song', another young man, bereft of family, knows he will be murdered before his next birthday.

Causley's third collection, *Union Street* (1957) secured his reputation as an important contemporary poet. Published with a preface by Edith Sitwell, then at the height of her influence, *Union Street* collected the best poems from Causley's first two volumes and added nineteen new ones, including three of his finest poems to date, 'I Am the Great Sun,' 'Innocent's Song,' and 'At the British War Cemetery, Bayeux,' the last of which Sitwell singled out for particular praise. In her preface, Sitwell placed Causley's work in its proper tradition, English folk song and ballad, but, while she praised Causley's traditional roots, she also notes his 'strange individuality.' Like most of Causley's admirer's, however, Sitwell had difficulty in explaining the appeal of his work. To express her approval Sitwell repeatedly fell back on vague exclamations of delight, such as 'beautiful,' 'deeply moving,' and the adjective which has followed Causley throughout his career, 'enchanting.' While these terms describe in some general way the effect Causley's poetry has on a sympathetic reader, they are so subjective that they shed little light on the nature of his literary achievement. Unfortunately, Sitwell's response typifies Causley's critical reception. His admirers have felt more comfortable in writing appreciations of his work than in discussing it in critical terms. This situation has given many critics unfamiliar with his work the understandable impression that while his poetry may be enjoyed, because of its simplicity, it does not bear serious analysis.

Causley's next four volumes continue to exploit the style he mastered in *Survivor's Leave* and *Union Street*. His poems remain exclusively in rhyme and meter, though he uses form with more overt sophistication to deal with his increasingly complex material. The ballad also continues to attract a major part of Causley's attention, though one now notices a more pronounced division in the kinds of ballads he writes. Each book contains the usual diverse mixture of poems on contemporary themes written in ballad meters, but there is always an additional group of strictly narrative ballads on remote historical or legendary subjects. While Causley had experimented with recreating folk ballads from his first book on, it now becomes a major preoccupation. In his introduction to his anthology, *Modern Ballads and Story Poems*, Causley confesses the basis of his fascination with 'the ancient virtues of this particular kind of writing.' The story poem or ballad, he writes, allows the poet to speak 'without bias or sentimentality.' It keeps the author from moralizing, but it 'allows the incidents of his story to speak for themselves; and, as we listen, we remain watchful for all kinds of ironic understatements.'

Causley seems to have seen these ballads—most of which were based on historical anecdotes or legends—as providing a balance of objectivity to the increasingly subjective and autobiographical poems he was also writing. While the war had provided Causley with a public subject matter in his early work, he now looked to these narrative ballads as creating another sort of accessible

31

common ground. In doing so Causley confirms his position as an outsider from the mainstream of twentieth-century poetry. His ballads rejected the then prevalent notion that a poet creates a private reality in the context of his own poems. Instead they deliberately make an appeal to common reality outside the poem.

While Causley's next three volumes present no stylistic break with the past, each of them marks a deepening of his thematic concerns. In *Johnny Alleluia* (1961) he explores his complex vision of Christ as the redeemer of mankind. Fully half the poems in this volume use Christ figures either explicitly, as in 'Cristo de Bristol' and 'Emblems of Passion,' or by implication, in strange transformations such as those in 'For an Ex-Far East Prisoner of War' and 'Guy Fawkes' Day,' where the effigy burning in the holiday fire becomes a redemptive sacrificial victim. Likewise Causley alternates scurrilous parodies of the Christ story, such as 'Sonnet to the Holy Vine' and the most disturbing 'Master and Pupil', with his most devout dedications. Reading his many treatments of the Christian drama, one sees that while Causley believes in the redemptive nature of Christ's sacrifice, he doubts man's ability to accept this divine love without betrayal.

Johnny Alleluia is also Causley's first volume which does not deal specifically with the war. While his concerns remain basically the same, they are now reflected in civilian themes, as in such vignettes of urban delinquents as 'My Friend Maloney' and 'Johnny Alleluia.' Only once does World War II literally come to haunt the present—in 'Mother, Get Up, Unbar the Door', where a woman's lover, killed nearly twenty years before at Alamein, returns from the grave to claim her daughter in a ghostly union. In this poem Causley shows remarkable skill at transposing a traditional ghost ballad into convincing contemporary terms. Causley also pursues his concern with the fall from innocence in 'Healing a Lunatic Boy', possibly his most vivid presentation of this central theme. In this poem a lunatic boy, who originally experiences the world in a direct way reminiscent of Adam in the Garden of Eden, is brought back to a mundane sense of reality by his cure.

In *Underneath the Water* (1968), Causley's most personal book of poems, he speaks frankly of both his childhood and adulthood. The poems about his boyhood are especially important in understanding his work, for, although he wrote a great deal of work about childhood earlier in his career, he rarely discussed his own. The childhood poems in *Underneath the Water* are therefore important for an understanding of the personal background of his most central themes. The volume opens with 'By St. Thomas Water', one of Causley's most complex views of the fall from innocence to experience. Two children (one of them presumably Causley himself), looking for a jar to fish with, steal one holding withered flowers on a tombstone. Before they go, they playfully decide to listen for the dead man's voice in the grave, and much to their horror, they think they hear him murmuring indistinctly underground. Noticing the tombstone's legend, 'He is not dead but sleeping,' they flee in terror. The narrator then spends the rest of his life wondering what the dead man tried to tell him.

In this volume Causley also gives several views of himself as an adult, especially as a teacher of the young—a vocation he finds problematic and frightening—in poems such as 'School at Four O'Clock' and 'Conducting a Children's Choir'. But the most disturbing view of his adult life comes in 'Trusham,' in which he revisits the village where his father and grandfather were born. He reads his dead father's name on the local war memorial, and even meets an old family acquaintance, who rebukes him for not marrying in order to carry on the family name. These experiences set off a crisis in the poet's mind which ends in a vision of his own cold and barren future.

Collected Poems (1975) solidified Causley's reputation in England and broadened his audience in America. The volume was widely reviewed on both sides of the Atlantic almost entirely in a positive light, but most reviewers presented Causley's achievement in a highly reductive manner. While they admired the ease and openness of his work and praised his unwavering commitment to narrative poetry, they did not find in their readings the resonance of language which distinguishes the finest poetry. By implication therefore they classified Causley as an accomplished minor poet, an engagingly eccentric antimodernist, who has mastered the traditional ballad at the expense of other work.

Most critics also missed the unexpected direction signalled by the twenty-three new poems in the collection. While continuing to work in rhyme and meter, Causley returned to free verse for the first time since *Farewell, Aggie Weston*, achieving uncharacteristic effects while liberating his talent for description. In 'Ten Types of

Hospital Visitor', which opens the "New Poems" section of his *Collected Poems*, Causley creates a detailed panorama of hospital life which unexpectedly modulates from realism to visionary fancy. In 'Ward 14' Causley uses free verse to achieve a painful directness in his description of a man visiting his brain-damaged old mother in the hospital. These poems demonstrate a richness of description and high degree of psychological naturalism not often found in Causley's earlier work.

But while mastering new techniques, Causley did not cease to regard traditional form as central to this work and he ends the *Collected Poems* with several formal poems, most notably 'A Wedding Portrait', one of his most important poems of self-definition. Here the poet's past and present, innocence and experience, are literally embodied in the scene of his middle-aged self looking at his parents' wedding photograph. His doomed father and mother appear hopeful and innocent in the portrait while the poet knows the subsequent pain they will undergo. His present knowledge cannot help them escape their plight, and he remains cut off from them now by time and death as absolutely as he was nonexistent to them on their wedding day. In a visionary moment Causley looks to his art to bridge the gap of time and restore both his dead parents to him and his lost childhood self to them. The *Collected Poems* therefore ends with this affirmation of poetry's power to triumph over death:

> I am a child again, and move
> Sunwards these images of clay,
> Listening for their first birth cry.
> And with the breath my parents gave
> I warm the cold words with my day:
> Will the dead weight to fly. To fly.

Causley's two most recent books, *Secret Destinations* (1984) and *Twenty-One Poems* (1986), ambitiously develop the new interests announced in his *Collected Poems*. Rather than retreating into one familiar style or set of subjects, Causley pursues a fascinating dialectic—both thematically and technically. Balancing the inner and outer worlds, he writes alternately of the past and present, the personal and the public, deliberately shifting his tone between the subjective and objective, while composing in both free and formal

34

verse. On the personal side Causley draws from memory a vivid series of family portraits depicting his grandparents,uncles, aunts, and cousins. While amplifying these personal poems with descriptions of his native town in characteristic pieces like 'Seven Houses' and 'On Launceston Castle', he also captures the foreign landscapes of his recent journeys to Canada and Australia. These travel poems strike a stark, objective note that contrasts to much of his earlier work. If old men should be explorers, few seem more adventurous than Charles Causley. At seventy he remains not only one of the most delightful poets in the language but also one of the most unpredictable.

With Dana Gioia, Hastings-on-Hudson, New York, 1984.(Photo by Christopher P. Stephens)

TWO FOR CHARLES

Roger McGough

1.

Outside a church at Launceston
St. Mary Magdalene sits up
And whenever the poet passes
Throws pebbles at him for luck.

For his poems are Christmas crackers
Filled with spells and charms.
Custard pies made with real custard.
Starry-gazy pies with real stars.
They sing out to be sung.

Making magic and music
Wherever he goes
He sits at the foot of England
And tickles its toes.

2.

Causley, God, the sea:
Cornish Trinity.

St. Mary Magdalene's, Launceston

LETTER TO CHARLES CAUSLEY

David Wright

Dear Charles, I write this doggerel
From Portingale to wish you well.
Here summer burns, and I am in
What has become my other home
Far from the borders of the north
Where half my heart is laid in earth;
Out of this window I can see
A uniting, dividing sea
While the red ground I tread upon
Recalls the land where I was born,
Fanatic sunlit Africa
Just half a horizon away.
Are you, as I hope I am, well?
And are you really seventy
Which, Deus vult, I soon shall be?
Do you remember how we met
In the studio of Patrick Swift
At midnight, and in Camden Town,
When, after pub-close, we burst in
With bottles and bonhomie to
Welcome our stranger guest, the new
Sweet chanter from the Cyprus Well,
The ballad-maker from Cornwall?
Our paths have seldom crossed since then,
And more than thirty years have gone
By us, but with exchanges of
Poems, admiration, and love;
And times have changed, and friends been lost,
Till our real future's now the past,
The treasure we laid up for age.
As memory is the truest Muse,
You will, dear Charles, with your clear voice
And fingers by long practice more
Skilful, if possible, than before,
Singing to the Apollonic lyre
Continue to delight, and draw
Articulate from the Cyprus Well
A music pure and natural.

A BIRTHDAY CARD

Philip Larkin

Dear CHARLES, My Muse, asleep or dead,
Offers this doggerel instead
To carry from the frozen North
Warm greetings for the twenty-fourth
Of lucky August, best of months
For us, as for that Roman once—
For you're a Leo, same as me
(Isn't it comforting to be
So lordly, selfish, vital, strong?
Or do you think they've got it wrong?),
And may its golden hours portend
As many years for you to spend.

One of the sadder things, I think,
Is how our birthdays slowly sink:
Presents and parties disappear,
The cards grow fewer year by year,
Till, when one reaches sixty-five,
How many care we're still alive?
Ah, CHARLES, be reassured! For you
Make lasting friends with all you do,
And all you write; your truth and sense
We count on as a sure defence
Against the trendy and the mad,
The feeble and the downright bad.
I hope you have a splendid day,
Acclaimed by wheeling gulls at play
And barking seals, sea-lithe and lazy
(My view of Cornwall's rather hazy)
And humans who don't think it sinful
To mark your birthday with a skinful.

Although I'm trying very hard
To sound unlike a birthday card,
That's all this is: so you may find it
Full of all that lies behind it—
Admiration; friendship too;
And hope that in the future you
Reap ever richer revenue.

CAUSLEY'S BALLADS

Stanley Cook

Charles Causley's ballads are so much a pleasure in themselves that it will not necessarily and may not easily occur to their admirer that they are a means of putting contemporary poetry in perspective. It is like a recent appearance of his on television: it was so much a pleasure to hear him *sing* his work that only afterwards could one think of the social and critical implications of this. Clearly there is the probability that at some time in the near future the work of Causley and other contemporary writers in the ballad form may be brought in from the margin of literary criticism to the centre. At such a time it will be seen, I think, that Causley not only sustained a great traditional form but also made characteristic and valuable developments in it. In particular, his best ballads have that quality peculiar to first-rate examples of their kind: that you can first meet them at ten or eleven but never grow out of them. In fact, though he has written some poems explicitly for children, it is usually when he is *not* writing for schools that he writes just the kind of poem that will succeed there.

The success of his ballads depends, irrespectively of his other powers, on a great gift. (My reader will guess I am going to name the silver spoon that all ballad poets have to be born to.) He is dramatic. For example, I feel that his masterpiece, 'The Song of Samuel Sweet', acts itself out in the mind's eye with beautifully managed fluctuations of story and interest and beautifully managed tension and is unforgettable. Verses 25 to 27 stir in their simpler way the same feelings as the fifth act of a Shakespearean tragedy. It is a feature of Causley's ballads that they leave you feeling you can see further than before, often much further, here for miles. A further example is the penultimate verse of 'Timothy Winters'. After an account of this boy's deprivations, we have

> At Morning Prayers the Master helves
> For children less fortunate than ourselves,
> And the loudest response in the room is when
> Timothy Winters roars 'Amen!'

40

and at this dramatic turn we feel the sands in the glass now running against *us*.

A comment of Causley's, in the *Poetry Book Society Bulletin*, No. 56, illuminates his combining traditional form with personal developments of it.

'"Simplify, simplify", wrote Thoreau. But at just what point does one stop, and allow suggestibility to take over? Every poem is a venture along a knife-edge towards that exact degree of simplification.'

Simplification tends to identification with the traditional ballads, one of which might begin, as a ballad of Causley's does, with

> It was a Sunday evening

and go on, as another ballad of Causley's does, with

> He wore no scarlet jacket
> Nor shirt of linen fine

and end, as a third ballad of Causley's does, with

> The other in green ground.

Apart from such verbal and rhythmic similarities, there is also the tendency to turn people and facts to legends. Even Timothy Winters and the modern 'wide boy', Maloney, are legends in their own time. Significantly Causley says of Timothy Winters, 'And they say there aren't boys like him any more.' I should say that the majority of Causley's ballads are on three classic ballad themes through the facts of each of which legend long since established a right of way: man's rejecting Christ, the sea's rejecting man and the unfairness of death. These themes he charges—with a pair of rich rhymes for spurs—with verve.

Between the confident rich rhymes (written in a time of free verse, pararhymes and assonance) Causley finds space for personal developments of his simple metre. I suggest that a poet writing fully rhymed verse is at his weakest or strongest not quite so much in his choice of rhymes as in his choice—when he already knows his rhymes—of what comes before them and fills out the

41

line. Take for example the first verse of Causley's 'The Statue of William the Conqueror, Falaise':

> See him ride the roaring air
> In an iron moustache and emerald hair,
> Furious with flowers on a foundry cob
> The bastard son of the late Lord Bob.

'Bastard' and 'late' are accurate; 'roaring' and 'furious', 'iron' and 'foundry', and 'emerald' are Causley. Take

> The coachman waits with a carriage and pair,
> But the bridegroom says, 'I won't be there,
> I don't care.'

and you have a conventional ballad. Prefix

> The bells assault the maiden air

and you have Causley; and have completed the first verse of his 'Ou Phrontis'. Causley says (*Poetry Book Society Bulletin*, No. 56):

'The effect of a poem (but not necessarily its "meaning", whatever that implies) should be instantaneous. At the same time, the poem should conceal certain properties that may only reveal themselves very gradually. The poem must have something in reserve; it must be capable of showing fresh aspects of its nature to reader as well as writer, perhaps over a period of years of reading and re-reading."

It is the unconventional adjectives and even more the unconventional verbs that you notice in re-reading Causley: hardness and violence—sea on granite.

The other considerable addition that I think Causley has made to the traditional use of the ballad form is his cultivated symbolism and, where he has scope, imagism. For example, everyday speech rhythm subtly highlights the symbolism of the last two lines of 'Ballad of the Bread Man'. In longer poems he finds scope to demand re-reading at verse length. He is, at intervals, an imagist, as in 'The Song of Samuel Sweet':

Rig the gallows, troopers!
        Make the ship shine!
Here's a likely cabin-boy
        For the death or glory line!
Give him a hempen collar
        As he heavenward steers,
The clouds about his ankles,
        The stars about his ears.

Is there any other poet who has written a verse like this in a ballad (and not impeded the narrative flow one jot)?

Causley is also a lyric poet. It seems to me that in lyric as in ballad he is at his best in realising a medieval tradition in contemporary terms. There is assured medieval simplicity incorporated in 'Shore Leave' and in 'Sailor's Carol', with its last verse of

Only the deep garden
Where green lilies grow,
The sailors rolling
In the sea's blue snow.

He has his own kind of war poetry, from his time in the Navy, which, he says, was the foundation of his poetry. It is a blend of intensity and panorama. See for example his 'Chief Petty Officer' with 'coal-burning soul'; and his '*HMS Glory* at Sydney, August 1945' in the vein of

                    there is no thrill
Like stepping ashore in a new country
With a clean shirt and with pound-notes in your pocket.

Union Street, which includes the last four poems I have referred to (in addition to 'Timothy Winters' and the ballad 'Nursery Rhyme of Innocence and Experience', which I feel sums up more than any other poem Causley's fascination with the sea), seems to me the best single volume of Causley's to look at. It is really three collections in one, since it includes poems from *Farewell Aggie Weston* and *Survivor's Leave*.

OUR FATHER

(for Charles Causley)

Bill Manhire

On one trip he brought home
a piece of stone from the river,
shaped like a child's foot

and filled with the weight
of the missing body. Another time
he just walked in

with our lost brother
high on his shoulders
after a two-day absence;

and it seems like only yesterday
he was showing us
the long pole, the one

out in the yard now,
taller than twice himself,
that still hoists

our mother's washing out of reach.

JERUSALEM

(For Charles Causley)

Chris Wallace-Crabbe

So Christ hiked in
along the dusty, serpentine
road from Bethany
deep in his early thirties
with hard hands,
gently imperious
as a grain of wheat.

So the hillslope welcome
was palmy and loud
but those who feathered power
knew the bubble emotion
for what it was,
even in the teeth of springtime, the heave of leaves.

Bent soldiers threw their dice
for a stained robe
in which the Roman law
would be all wrapped up
for yellow centuries.

Bits of that cross
sparkled like glass
in every brother's eyeball:
nobody on earth
can put it together again.

AS NEW AS IT IS OLD

Ronald Tamplin

Albert Camus writes in his wartime *Carnets:*

> The consolation of this world is that there are no continuous
> sufferings. A grief disappears and a joy is reborn. They
> all balance out. Ours is a world of compensations.

and, again a few pages on:

> Plague. There are at the moment distant ports whose
> water is pink at sunset.

Charles Causley too expresses this sense of an enigmatic world
which suffers but is capable, though uncertainly, of consolation:

> I do not know if anyone is here.
> If so, if not so, I must let it be.
> I hold your drifted hand; no time to tell
> What six dead women hear, or whom they see.
>
> *'Six Women'*

Even within his comedy, by turns delicate and rumbustious, there
is a frequent and profound sense of the hurt of the world. It is not
felt primarily as it impinges on the poet directly but rather as he
observes it acting on others. Sometimes the poems seem to share
T. S. Eliot's or rather Julian of Norwich's medieval hope that 'all
shall be well,' but the assumption is never lightly made, nor is it
consistently or characteristically there. Causley is his own man
and does not give himself easily to solutions of mere social habit or
tickets-of-leave. His normal stance is to celebrate the dignity and
strength of men, women and creatures in the face of the hurt and
loss endemic in their world.

> The torn tramp, rough with talents, walks the park,
> Children have swift stones ready. Men, dogs, bark.
> The light falls on the bay, the cold sea leaks,
> The slate face flushes, opens its lips, speaks.

46

> In from the moor the pointing shadows flock,
> Finger, beneath the river, the pure rock

he writes in 'A Short Life of Nevil Northey Burnard'. The excitement of Causley's poetry begins in such compassionate observation. It brings with it a defiant, even surreal joy:

> Three Wise Men wait at my garden gate
> My crown is crooked, but my jacket is strait.
>> *'The Ballad of Billy of Nosey Bent'*

There are no short cuts to affirmation. It is reached, if it is, through pain, solitude, madness and loss, through a Romantic extension of Milton's 'tested virtue'.

Indeed it might be felt that Causley's solutions are Romantic solutions. He demonstrates a profound sense of the ultimate loneliness of man within a busy human scene:

> Though we sail the seas together
> Each of us must sail alone.
>> *'Nelson Gardens'*

The visionary world of the mad is preferred to mundane or miraculous cure in 'Healing a Lunatic Boy':

> On a stopped morning
>> The city spoke,
> In my rich mouth
>> Oceans broke.
> No more on the spun shore
>> I walked unfed.
> I drank the sweet sea,
>> Stones were bread.
>
> Then came the healer
>> Grave as grass,
> His hair of water
>> And hands of glass.
> I watched at his tongue
>> The white words eat,
> In death, dismounted
>> At his stabbed feet.

He sees art and imagination as heroic in themselves:

> May your daughters wear like diamonds
> > Their virtue at their throats,
> May your sons, like brave sea-bandits,
> > Never take to the boats.
>
> Only the fool or the poet
> > Cuts down the flashing tree
> To burn its belly with fire
> > And take to the jealous sea.
>
> > > *'Serenade to a Cornish Fox'*

The mythic imagination seizes meaning from an inchoate world:

> Set forth so, imagination!
> > Loot the locked turrets of light,
> Speak with the tongues of bandits and angels,
> > Put winter to flight.
>
> > > *'Legend'*

He celebrates the poets, among them Keats and Clare, and the insights of children. These are all Romantic preoccupations but with Causley they have a quizzicality and irony that only Byron, among the Romantics, displays. In modern times Causley's nearest neighbours are Auden, Roy Campbell and Louis Mac-Neice and it is Auden he celebrates in 'Letter from Jericho'.

> Auden, born public exchanger of winks
> At empty solemnities,
> For fifty years a seasoner of thought
> With seafuls of necessary salt,
> Sounding tirelessly against the thumping walls of cant,
> And affirming the civilized virtues
> With an unshadowed tongue, meanwhile declaring
> The private, shy and loving heart—

It is this sense of man both public and private in his responsibilities and needs that seems to be crucial in Causley's thought. In his world all men are islands sustained in being by their natural dignity and islanded because a man's central knowledge is his own and inalienable. The gaps between us are bridged by the ability to sympathise and help and, in the particular case of the poet, to observe and celebrate. In fact it is this sense of his own separation that actually forces man to make these compassionate links and bridges between 'solitaries/Like most of us'. There are exceptions who unselfconsciously perceive the solidarity of humankind and, without adverting to it, act upon it. Ma Treloar is such a one sheltering her 'rubble of children' 'like sprats/In an enveloping ocean'. And not only her children:

> 'Lord, man,' she'd say, 'but you've certainly
>   Grown thinner,'
> As the prophet of the desert, having eaten nothing
>   but sand and prayers for a week
>   Arrived for Sunday dinner,
> Leaving his taut, ex-ravening lion with its umbrella
>   of bones and skin
>   At the foot of the stair,
> Doves descending on its pecked head as it lay
>   With the gentle vulture, the lynx, the once
>   wild-eyed hare.
>
>   *'Demolition Order'*

The world which Causley supposes is not an ideal one that cannot be realised but an actual one that exists. In it the introvert and the extrovert lie down together. Ma Treloar enacts it but each man is that world in himself. Causley's poetry is about the recognition and acceptance of our own constituent natures, emblematically conceived as a duality within us. Jack O'Lent seeks out the Galilee man, Herod double-talks 'Out of the Christmas Fire', the Chief Petty Officer's 'narrow forehead' is 'ruffled by the Jutland wind'. This self-knowledge is achieved within the erosion that man daily suffers, in sight of the frozen face, lying

> ... his eyes quarried by glittering fish,
> Staring through the green freezing sea-glass
> At the Northern Lights.
>
>   *'Convoy'*

and in sight of the primal and ultimate sea, emblem at once of death and love:

By the crunching, Cornish sea
Walk the man and walk the lover,
Innocent as fish that fare
In the high and hooking air,
And their deaths discover.

'Grave by the Sea'

And so, enigmatically as ever, in 'On the Border':

'What is that land,' you said, 'beyond
Where the river bends the meadow?'

and in the morning:

We saw what we could see.
No Man's Land was no man's land.
It was the sea.

With such conjoined and resolving opposites at work in it
Causley's poetry has an.oddly medieval dimension. I say oddly
because, if it is there, it is totally updated. There is nothing folksy
or antiquarian or Pre-Raphaelite about it. The medieval world
capable of resolution and redemption is filtered through a
modern sensibility with our own profound sense of multiplicity
and chaos. To that extent it is disabled but it is still powerful. In
the past Causley has tended to use those echoes of the medieval
world that persist in the folk imagination. And he has used with a
sure insight that most public form, the ballad, to enshrine the
most private intensities. More recently in 'St Martha and the
Dragon' and *The Gift of a Lamb* he has reinvigorated more strictly
medieval forms—the saint's legend and the mystery play. With
his most recent work, *The Ballad of Aucassin and Nicolette*, he has
turned to medieval romance. This stage presentation with music
by Stephen McNeff was specially commissioned by South West
Music Theatre and played extensively in the West Country as
well as in London.

Aucassin and Nicolette is an anonymous thirteenth-century
French romance of great distinction. It mixes verse and prose,
romantic lyric and grotesque humour and is full of refreshing and
varied incident. In the original story Aucassin, son of the Count
of Beaucaire in Provence, is prostrated by his love for Nicolette, a
slave-girl bought from the Saracens by the local Viscount. The

50

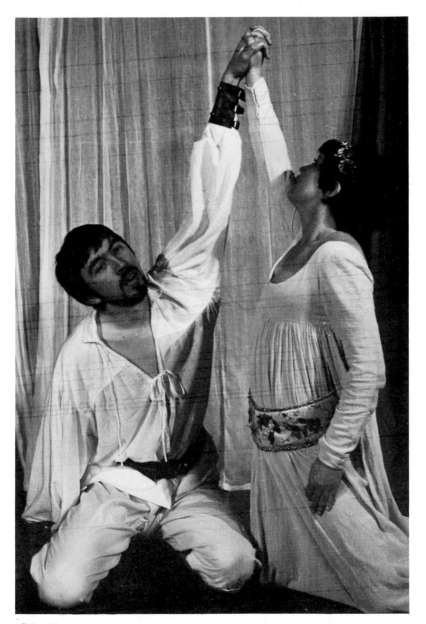

Robert Karas and Paula Bent in the title rôles. ('The Ballad of Aucassin & Nicolette', 1978)

Count is exasperated. He needs Aucassin to help him fight a war and drops a hint to the Viscount to get Nicolette out of the way. She is imprisoned in the Viscount's tower. Aucassin agrees to fight if he can meet Nicolette afterwards. He captures Bougars of Valence, the Count's enemy, in battle but releases him when the Count fails to keep his bargain over Nicolette. The Count imprisons Aucassin. Nicolette escapes and hides in a wood. When she is reported as lost Aucassin is released and goes in search of her. He goes to the same wood and there meets the character who, much enhanced, becomes Causley's vivid Martin Oxboy. The lovers meet and, after a journey by sea, reach Torelore, a Topsy-Turvy land. They are captured by Saracens and separated, Aucassin to be shipwrecked off the coast of Provence. His parents have died and Beaucaire is his. Meanwhile Nicolette is revealed as the King of Carthage's daughter. Disguised as a minstrel she returns to Beaucaire and is eventually reunited with Aucassin.

Causley's decision to update *Aucassin and Nicolette* is a happy one. The unusual mixture of prose and verse in the original gives full rein to his own metrical skill and love of variety. The episodic manner of medieval romance fits well with Causley's inventiveness and feeling for larger-than-life characters. The topsy-turvy kingdom of Torelore lends itself to surreal comedy. Above all the quest of the lovers in search of each other fits in with Causley's own questing approach to the world as well as his celebration of the need for human love. The critic Rosemond Tuve once said, talking about medieval allegorical interpretations, that there was only one theme, loss and salvation. In a sense the remark is capable of much wider application. Perhaps all stories are in the end about loss and salvation. In any case loss by separation and salvation through love both occur in the story of Aucassin and Nicolette and they are important correlates in Causley's work taken as a whole. The medieval plot also involves ballad singers and sea-journeys and so gives natural place to two of his particular skills. It is all vintage Causley with a timeless verbal quality that is never pastiche or 'historical'. The theatrical verve never lets up and at the same time quiet and reflective elements in the love quest are allowed full play. Causley proves to be particularly good at handling medieval-style recognition scenes:

Whose is the ship that I sail in?
The King of Carthage
Carthage King.

Who are these sailors about me stand?
Sons of the King
Of Carthage land.

Why do they wear the silk and pearl?
Half are Princes
And half are Earls.

Why do they make much joy of me?
They once had a sister—
Stolen was she.

Was she a mother or was she a maid?
Stolen she was
As a little babe.

The comic swashbuckling of Count Garin and the Saracen Tarik is also very well handled and the staging with a small cast doubling the parts was extremely inventive in the performance I saw. *The Ballad of Aucassin and Nicolette* extends Charles Causley's formal range and confirms the breadth of his art as we already know it. Characteristically in Causley's work imagination fuses the materials of fancy so that the least action touches the springs of all action. In *The Ballad of Aucassin and Nicolette* Martin Oxboy expresses starkly and simply the paradoxical duality that Causley is witness to:

(AUCASSIN goes. OXBOY watches his departure open-mouthed. Gazes at coins; puts them in his pouch. As he is about to move off, he spots a moth pitched on his club. He observes it for a moment: an air of menace. Then quietly:)

OXBOY: Moth! Moth!
                Light as breath.
            Here is life.
            Here is death.

53

(He removes it from the club: holds it in his hand)

> Wing, moth! And higher!—
>   To moon and star;
> Kinder these are
>   Than human fire.

(He watches it flutter up and away)

In the fluttering moth and in the closing verse of the play the Romance spirit and Causley's own reserved optimism in spite of known odds seem to coincide:

> For the tale that we have told
> Is as new as it is old;
> It is far and it is near,
> Never was, yet it is here.
> It is fable, it is true,
> It is me, and it is you;
> Here now ended, yet it starts
> Ever in the human heart,
> And is story of our play.

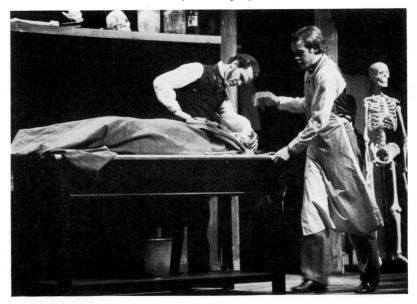

Jonathan Smedley (left) and Christopher Martin (right) in 'The Doctor and the Devils', The Banff Centre, Alberta, 1984.

LITTORAL

(for Charles Causley)

Lawrence Sail

Out past the salt rhines
Where the ocean lopes and flows,
Time is pure alien theatre,
A movement of lights blazing
Into distance that slows to texture,
The lustrous layers of haze.

But here at the clifftop's edge
Under ice the water bleeds
Drop by drop, grim measure
Of each second leaching
Through fine pipettes to fall
To the dead acoustic of the beach.

Your ground is richly between -
By the footlights of foam, where one
Well-sealed bottle distils
No message but its own
Bright vintage air. Out to sea,
Calmly the ships go on.

THE POETRY OF CHARLES CAUSLEY

Edward Levy

Union Street, which appeared in 1957, might be said to pre-figure Charles Causley's *Collected Poems:* 1951–1975. There too the poems of previous collections had been gathered in, with a group of new poems forming the final section of the book. Edith Sitwell's enthusiastic preface to the earlier collection suggests that Causley had graduated to the communion of inspired mid-century bards—Dylan Thomas, Sidney Keyes—whose praises she had earlier sung so generously. While *Collected Poems* has no such preface, it has been universally approved—by the deferential as well as the warmly appreciative. John Fuller, in his *Times Literary Supplement* review, didn't disguise his impatience with some Causley qualities, yet rounded off in these terms: 'But however [Causely] develops, this book stands as a tribute to an essential function of verse: the power to enchant.'

Such remarks are, I think, notably vague compared with Causley's own authoritative, sometimes gnomic, but always tough utterances about his poetry and poetry in general. There is a danger that in the case of a poet such as Causley, his evident 'power to enchant' may be seized on as a means of glossing over the complexities in his canon of work; so that he remains no more than a canny eccentric, an encouraging entertainer. Alternatively, an admirer of the Sitwellian kind may be equally unsatisfactory—the poet who enchants remaining no more than the inspired, enchanting poet. In fact, the words 'enchant' and 'charm' are central to Causley's work; but their full meaning may only be understood through a close reading of the poems.

Causley has insisted that 'The mere fact of a poem appearing simple in language and construction bears no relation whatsoever to the profundity of ideas it may contain'; and 'A Ballad for Katharine of Aragon', an early poem which seems to me to contain the central theme of his work, bears out this contention. The poem mourns the fates of an infanta dispatched from home to an arranged, politically expedient marriage to a king who subsequently rejected her, and of the poet's boyhood companion

56

killed in the 1939 war. The fortunes of Jumper Cross and Kate reflect a passage from innocence to painful experience, and from love to lovelessness. Causley employs the juxtaposition of different tenses afforded by the ballad form—narrative past with lyric or aphoristic present—to bring the two together across the centuries. The correspondence of their fates is given poignant emphasis in the final image of them as a courting couple united in the common lovelessness that has severed them from other human beings, in Katharine's case the lovelessness implicit in the disparity between a young woman's romantic hopes and the course of her marriage, in Jumper's the homicidal lovelessness of war. The last stanza of the ballad runs as follows:

> O shall I leap in the river
> And knock upon paradise door
> For a gunner of twenty-seven and a half
> And a queen of twenty four?
> From the almond tree by the river
> I watch the sky with a groan,
> For Jumper and Kate are always out late
> And I lie here alone.

The poem provides a useful way into Causley's work as a whole. It gives us a world of lovelessness, violence, indifference and disappointment, associating these with images of cold—'the frozen fen', 'the cold stone chest'. There are, also, such effects as that of the accusing precision of Jumper's age. But equally important, it shows us the poet as survivor, washed up, as it were, confronting this state of affairs. He appears in this last verse hopelessly left out in the cold: at the simple idiomatic level this phrase holds, if we keep in mind the final image of Jumper and Kate as a courting couple who leave the poet alone every night— the metaphor is remarkable in that it does work in two directions. Causley figures as the third in a desolate trinity, having at the outset of his poetic career to face his separation from the dead, and to combat an external world of human lovelessness, and the enervating, isolating effect of that world on him personally. The poem provides a platform for both a public and a private poetry.

Nor is it simply a post-Second World War poetry. Causley has from the start been concerned with childhood, sometimes very early childhood, and the period of his childhood was immediately after the 1918 Armistice. Moreover, his father was dying from the effects of German gas in Causley's first seven years. Whether the small son was much aware of this at the time or not, it was at any rate a fact he had to recognize later. Poems such as 'On Seeing a Poet of the First World War on the Station at Abbeville', and the last poem in *Collected Poems*, 'A Wedding Portrait', would support a contention that the First World War is as important to Causley as the Second. At any rate, lovelessness and loss are associated in his mind with both.

Causley's work seems to grow from a meditation on the predicament we are left with at the close of 'A Ballad for Katharine of Aragon'. There is an explicit awareness of the anonymous, multiple dead, particularly in the early poems; while many of the ballads have as their theme disappointed expectations—the disappointment either wistful or desolate. And the high hopes Causley's characters have are blighted either by death or a cheating disappearance of love. This is associated with an innocence which is in turn, as the poetry develops, associated with the New Testament concept of grace. Primarily the Bible gives Causley a vocabulary: the occasional epiphanic visions and consequent states of grace that we read of in his poems depend on his witnessing simplicity and wholeness in the behaviour of human beings. A recent poem, 'At Kfar Kana', is a case in point. The only kind of after-life offered in the poems is through the dedemptive power of memory and the quickening of human affection.

There are times when these are absent or simply not enough. In 'At the British War Cemetery, Bayeux' Causley acknowledges the brute fact of annihilation, the 'jigsaws of impossible bone': the poet's offerings to the anonymous 'five thousand' under the earth fall hopelessly short of 'the one gift you cannot give'. And this hopelessness applies to the poet's idea of himself as survivor; appearing fitfully throughout *Collected Poems*: indeed this candour is particularly moving because it punctuates a body of work in which the poet is often defiantly gay or lightly self-teasing. Witness 'Hospital', which begins with the numb, jerked out lines:

> Hospital is the war again.
> I left my clothes somewhere in town.
> Here I am innocent and good.

The sense of isolation, arising from a feeling of redundancy or vulnerability, belongs also to childhood. In 'Reservoir Street', Causley evokes an episode from his own childhood. He was the victim of the negating spitefulness of his town cousins. In 'Conducting a Children's Choir', Causley, as schoolmaster, recognizes the potential for brutality and suffering in the children he conducts. And it is worth noting that the line in 'Hospital', 'Here I am innocent and good', begs the question of what Causley is 'there'.

Causley, like Dickens, expresses his antipathy to moral emptiness or corruption in strongly physical terms. An empty ritual is pervaded by a nauseous miasma. In 'Death of a Poet', his valediction to MacNeice, the church is filled with 'the stench of flowers', the spray of flowers compared to rays of a sun which chills rather than warms. And this miasma extends to corrupted human beings, who are represented, in a markedly Dickensian manner, as monster or monument. It is no doubt a Tommy tactic to cock a snook at the enemy by means of this kind of cartoonery; and Tommy humour owes much to Dickens. But in Causley as in Dickens, we have more than slapstick ridicule, though there is something of this as well. The grotesque is disarmed only so long as one has the whip-hand; and the poet is by no means sure that he has this. The wholeness that both Causley and Dickens regret is undermined constantly by the vicious emptiness of public and private action.

For Causley, poetry is a weapon of attack against these forces. If in 'A Ballad for Katharine of Aragon' the speaker watches the sky 'with a groan', in 'Death of a Poet' the lines occur: 'I looked in the wet sky for a sign but no bird descended./I went across the road to the pub; wrote this.' Writing a poem is seen here as simply the best thing Causley can do in the circumstances. But from the start, Causley has seemed to know exactly what he is doing in his poems: remarkably self-aware; conscious of what excites him, choosing the area that excites him most as his home. In an early poem we have him characteristically spinning an emotional coin between nostalgia for the distant foreign parts encountered during the war and the native Cornwall to which he has returned: 'Here by the Inney, nature has her city:/(O the cypress trees of Mohamed Ali Square!)'. The coin settles on the Cornwall face: 'The children build their harbour in the meadow/And the crystal lark floats in the Cornish air.' Any myth of air, water, earth and fire that figures in the poems as an attempt to redeem the dead and image this redemption is rooted in Causley's conscious adherence to the particular air, water and earth he has known since childhood: the Cornish air, the sea off Cornwall, the rivers Inney and Tamar, the stream running by St Thomas's churchyard in Launceston. The changes he rings on the four elements reflect his vision and the progress of his meditation.

Such imaginative concentration is, I think, much more than the rapture of Causley's lunatic boy who regrets a world where 'Trees turned and talked to me/Tigers sang,/Horses put on leaves,/Water rang'. Causley has, admittedly, endorsed the boy's regret, remarking in interview: 'Perhaps his condition was as bad as that of the poet who has had his gift taken away from him'. But this is only half Causley's story. Poetic imagination is rooted in experience, in the experience of a world in which, though not in a muzzling, positivist sense, 'river *is* river/And tree *is* tree' (my italics). Indeed river is particular river to Causley; and everywhere in his work there is the impulse to name, to particularize. The poet redeems matter by naming it, casts a spell by spelling out. In 'A Ballad for Katharine of Aragon' the image of the farmers' boots on Kate's memorial slab suggests the wearing away of the inscription, and so, oblivion; while 'A Short Life of Neville Northey Burnard', Causley's poetic biography of the nineteenth-century Cornish sculptor, is itself a kind of sustained epitaph, beginning, 'Here lived Burnard. . .'.

In this poem Causley writes that Burnard himself 'turned, as Midas, men to stone, then gold./Forgot, he said, what it was to be cold.' The transforming activity suggested here applies not just to the matter an artist deals with, nor only to those whose forms he would revive and perpetuate, but to the artist himself. And Causley seems in his work to be attempting to remedy the cold separation from the dead that he feels as he attempts to redeem them by love for them. If he is unusually self-aware, recognizing and working from his affections, he is also attempting throughout his collections to get his bearings. The final poems of individual collections suggest this. If we deal *Collected Poems* into its original suits we find poems of self-recognition are the final poems. 'Grave by the Sea' and 'Who?', the last poems in *Johnnie Alleluia* (1961) and *Figgie Hobbin* (1970) respectively, are just such poems. They act as epigraphs to the collections, in some measure illuminating the poems which precede them. 'Grave by the Sea' concludes:

> Now in the speaking of the sea
> He waits under the written stone,
> And kneeling at his freezing frame
> I scrub my eye to see his name
>
> And read my own.

The poem 'Who?' ends with a question provoked by the vision of a young boy: 'Why does he say that his name is my own?' The question is both rhetorical and straight, conveying at once recognition and perplexity.

If we assume that poems dealing with the poet's own identity are intentionally placed at the end of each collection, then the last poem in *Collected Poems* must take an extra burden too. And, though markedly Larkinesque in style, 'A Wedding Portrait' does bring together all the major strands of Causley's work. Like 'A Ballad for Katharine of Aragon', it painfully contrasts innocence and experience. Where, in the earlier poem, two historical times were brought together through the juxtaposition of tenses, here the trick with time a photograph plays serves a similar purpose; more properly, it is what occasions the poem. The innocent love that Causley's parents have for one another on their wedding day is contrasted with the murderousness of war; their apparent blindness to reality with the reality of:

> the lean
> Year of the *Lusitania*; gas
> Used at the Front. Arras and Ypres
> More than place-names. 1915.

It is enhanced by Causley's awareness, sixty years later, of mass annihilation and burial under sea and earth; also—though he makes no mention of it—with his knowledge that his father died from the effects of gas. Just as the 'I' figure lies 'here alone' at the end of the earlier ballad, so in this poem Causley the son is 'not here'—on that day in 1915 he simply doesn't exist. Yet the poem turns on the reflection that 'man is a breath/And at the end lies in the fire,/In bolting water, or the earth.' We have the impression of

61

a dormant, hidden reality, the apparently impotent, fleeting 'breath' becoming, by a play on the word, a means of uncovering this reality. The poem ends with these lines:

> I am a child again, and move
> Sunwards these images of clay,
> Listening for their first birth-cry.
> And with the breath my parents gave
> I warm the cold words with my day:
> Will the dead weight to fly. To fly.

Causley is restored to his parents' love for him, not just by the bridge that his meditation builds across the decades, but by a forward motion in time. Causley, on that day in 1915 not even a thought, became his parents' child a few years later. The breath given him he sees in terms of a latent element which, activated, can make sense of and join in unity with others. Causley is quite clear about what this is: it is the poet's breath which can, by naming and defining, bring both dead and living to life, reminding the living of the dead and healing the deadness in them. Like 'A Ballad for Katharine of Aragon', the poem is both an elegy and an account of the poet's own condition. Unlike the earlier poem, it defines the means of recovering loss and, by careful definition and appellation is itself an instrument of recovery.

Not that 'A Wedding Portrait' does this single-handed. Causley's strength lies in the abundance and variety of his work, in the spontaneity which makes possible the changes of register which we find there, in his capacity for making poems in different registers, sometimes for adults, sometimes for adults and children. When his poems echo other poets, this is deliberate and explicit: evidence of his sense of poetic fellowship, and of his confidence. He has remained true to himself, turning his attention only to what he finds compelling and meaningful. It strikes me that he is considerably more sure-footed in this respect than most of his contemporaries. At a time when many poets feel compelled to find roots, to seek out their childhood, Causley, staying more or less completely put in Cornwall, doesn't experience this problem. No doubt he was lucky to be rooted from the start. But an awareness of roots is a subjective matter, and a sense of where the ore of poetic insight lies is primarily a question of how deeply things matter to a poet. No doubt Causley's experiences in the Navy in the Second World War, apart from enriching his poetic vocabulary, clarified for him just how deep his roots ran. The first poem of Causley's first collection, *Farewell, Aggie Weston*, and of his *Collected Poems*, is 'Keats at Teignmouth'. And one of Keats's disclosures is, I think, apposite in any discussion of Causley. His achievement is the result of his trusting more firmly than most in 'the holiness of the heart's affections and the truth of the imagination.'

WHAT THE ROSE SAID

(for Charles Causley)

Peter Levi

I am the rose of summer nuzzling spring
half hidden in light green, smelt before seen,
consumed in one breath, withered opening,
a pod of prickles where a rose has been:
when the storm shatters it the thrush will sing,
then by moonlight the nightingale will lean
a dying breast on the dry thorn singing
music as complicated and as clean
as the bird loving, the rose flourishing,
but not what roses or what poems mean,
because the blood corrupted melts the sting
and words die on the tongue, rose unfolding
melts his whole spice in one refreshing fume
which no songbird or poem can exhume.

FAREWELL, FOR CHARLES CAUSLEY

Colin MacInnes

I first met Charles Causley when we were both imprisoned by warfare—he an unreluctant mariner, I an unarmed warrior—on the three-by-threequarter mile rock of Gibraltar: an experience by which none who endured it have been left unmarked; for the paradox of sunlight, no black-out by night, and shops groaning with propaganda goods in the only remaining allied foothold on the European mainland, accompanied an exclusively male society (except for eighteen, I think, Wrens), the tantalizing daily spectacle of forbidden Spain, and for most of us locked up there, a two-year stint to do.

When we met again in England, Charles had already become what, from birth, he always must have been, a poet; and one for whose verses I felt then and have done increasingly (were that possible), as his great gifts have matured, a total admiration. Some have been deceived by the 'simplicity' of Causley's forms, and by his obsession with many timeless themes—especially those of the sea, of death, of enduring love and of quickly passing youth—into supposing he was a 'regional natural': not at once perceiving that these eternally recurring human situations had been given new life in terms of our own times; and that the 'ballad style' had always been manipulated by a consummate and extremely contemporary technician. Yet for all its art and skill, what it most compelling and endearing about Charles Causley's poetry is that heavenly gift which he possesses of effusion: of singing like a bard from the mind, heart, and soul, certainly, and also with a perpetual siren voice that first sang somewhere in Greece, in Egypt, and in Eden.

This splendid poet, Cornish by intuition, Devonian by sagacity, has honoured me with his friendship and by a constantly solicitous vigilance of criticism and encouragement that enables anyone who dreams into words to feel that one ear, at least, is listening, even when he may think there are no others.

TO A POET WHO HAS TRAVELLED: REFLECTIONS ON THE RECENT POETRY OF CHARLES CAUSLEY

Barry Newport

In 1976, the year after the publication of his much-praised *Collected Poems*, Charles Causley took early retirement from teaching in order to devote more time to writing. Since then we have had a number of anthologies, stories and verse for children, verse-plays and translations, not to mention many book and periodical contributions. More importantly, the poems have kept coming, collected as *Secret Destinations* in 1984 and an interim collection, *21 Poems*, published as a limited edition in 1986 by the Celandine Press. During these eleven years his work has shown a stylistic broadening, apparent in certain of the new poems at the end of the *Collected*, leading to a more descriptive kind of poem in rhymed speech rhythms or free verse, as well as an increasing variety of traditional forms. It is very different compared with what we have been used to seeing, but to me the breaking free from the rather tight patterns of his earlier work has been an important development. Language, and the increasingly personal experience it is translating, have become more closely related.

Secret Destinations, which I shall be discussing chiefly, represents another departure in that, while a number of poems continue to relate to people and places in Cornwall, the great majority have arisen from travel in Europe, Canada and Australia where Causley has had a number of reading tours and longer engagements in the last seven years or so. Often the scenery is strange and colourful, but Causley is not a poet 'on location' (many of the poems were not written till long after), nor is he writing a verse travelogue. 'For myself', he said on a radio broadcast, 'it is very necessary that the scene and setting of a poem should somehow fuse with the personal life, be at one with it.' In 'Cottesloe Beach', as I suspect in most cases, what we are looking at is a transmutation of past experience. In the dark of late evening the sound of the sea evokes memories of the terror of wartime:

> Within the sea's dark voice I hear
> Another's, long unvisited.
> Sleepless, I listen for the light,
> The star still shining in my head.

'Bankhead' is a ghost-town, once a small mining community, in Alberta: a remote, quiet ruin: 'The unmade engine-house a mix/ of little stones and children's bricks;/Torn rail tracks, giant cacti; paths/From nowhere to nowhere ...'. Another desolate landscape, both external and internal, is 'Glen Helen', a place in the red-hot interior of Australia. With superb precision the poem describes a desert sunrise:

> Divider-stiff, wading birds stab the map
> Of corrugated water. The day's finger
> Sharpens the skeletons of the ranges: crouched
> Frilled lizards, frozen dinosaurs ...

What this imagery corresponds to is the painful death of a relationship:

> Pretended not to notice how love bled
> Into the eager sand. Lay, heart on heart:
> Yet never slept so cold, so far apart.

Love and separation enter many of Causley's poems, though the vision is not always as bleak in other types of poem or when he is writing at one remove from his own immediate experience. 'Bamboo Dance' describes a dance, performed by a Filipino couple, in which the feet are placed sometimes between, sometimes outside, clashing bamboo poles in time to music that gradually increases in tempo. The joys of love are expressed with flowing movement: 'It is as if they swim in air/Music, like water, bears them up.' What they are borne up from are the perils that are inextricably bound up with love; here in a moment of tender observation, the dancers emerge unscathed, though the thought is, I think, still retained in the contrasting 'locked' and 'gentle' in the last line of the poem: 'Smiling, the dancers go,/Hand locked in gentle hand, their way.'

Elsewhere, we see a readiness to try out fresh ideas, though always within the needs of the poem. Here is an example of

66

Causley's technical ingenuity: an adaptation of Longfellow to describe a menacing Aborigine dance:

> Beaded and in
> feather bracelets
> to the hoarse-voiced didge-
> ridoo,
> they were emu
> and echidna,
> swirling snake and kang-
> aroo

In one or two poems there is a new colloquial informality. 'Pinchgut', for instance, takes in this tourist slogan: 'Famed for Fun since 31,/Seven miles from Sydney/And a thousand miles from care'. And he notes under a health warning : 'Kiss a non-smoker/and enjoy the difference'. These might seem to be gratuitously funny note-book jottings, but what they are reflecting is a feeling of spiritual aridity. 'I am seeking a sign/Any kind of sign'; but what he finds is a piece of graffiti which 'a moving hand has written': '*Jesus Jogs*'. While this is not one of his best poems it does show a truth to experience, even a negative one.

Religious themes are certainly not lacking, however. 'At the Church of St Anthony, Lisbon' tells us about the Saint '. . . for whom/The wild ass knelt before the Host as witness/To Christ within the Eucharist . . .' and at whose death bells rang of their own accord. These and other details of the Saint's story make the poet question his own disbelief. But the bells are silent, and a passing donkey 'ballasted with guttering' stops but does not kneel. Legend alone cannot be a key to Faith, yet the mood of the poem suggests that the door is far from locked. In 'Flying', the scene shifts to Seville and the Easter *pasos*: 'the squealing bands', 'porters shouldering wounded Jesus down/Holy Week', 'the Holy Virgin . . . her shaken crown/a foliage of stars, her wax tears spent'. Someone adjusts the soldier's lance and fixes Pilate's cloak. As in some of Causley's earlier poems, Christ is seen as a sacrificial redeemer, betrayed here by twentieth-century carnival. The poet has come with the thirst of a pilgrim, but what he is offered is a drink of coke from a gypsy vendor who 'sees me for what I was, for what I am.' He is, in the end, a tourist; but in their thought and feeling both these poems are religious and are among the best religious poems he has written.

The first group of poems in *Secret Destinations* contains a number of what might loosely be termed 'Portraits', following on from 'Silent Jack' and 'A Wedding Portrait' at the end of the *Collected Poems*. 'Grandmother' is about an old Sudeten woman in Germany, a refugee in Hitler's thirties: '... her history/Carried in paper bags beneath each arm ...' She is seen as a metaphor for that period of European upheaval, and portrayed as neither good nor evil: '... both heaven and hell/Entirely unprepared for her arrival.' Other characters are drawn from a seemingly inexhaustible store of childhood mythology: Richard Bartlett, the quarryman, killed by a falling piece of slate, and Uncle Stan, who enlisted in the Canadian army and died in Canada. An aunt, called Dora, is plain, resilient and god-fearing: 'Bullets for fingers, hair cut like a man,/Feet in a prophet's sandals ...' We learn about a tragedy from her own childhood, her reticence in talking about her innermost feelings and her lack of fear when she died:

> Our only death, said Dora, is our first.
> And she turned from me. But her winter eye
> Spoke every word that I had left unread.

As in the other poems, the poet is not simply giving us a photograph. What he is reading in that 'winter eye' is a prophesy of his own death.

The few poems relating more directly to Cornwall include one or two from the later '70's, a period when Charles Causley felt the need, I think, to reassess his life and the town in which nearly all of it had been spent. In a 1977 article in *The Listener* he mentioned a Canadian expatriate writer who, while being shown round Launceston, had said: 'the difference between you and me is that you know where you'll be buried.' 'He may well be right', Causley wrote, 'but what concerns me more is that I should never fall into the trap of thinking life in my parish unchanging'. 'Seven Houses' is an exploration of that theme; in it different parts of the poet's life are symbolically related in turn to 'the house where I was born', but in the end that house, like everything else, will decay and vanish. 'On Launceston Castle', dating from about 1980, gives us a panoramic view of the town, but what we are really looking at are metaphors expressing the uncertainty the poet felt in interpreting his surroundings. There is nothing uncertain about the quality of the poem itself however, and no doubt either that its last stanza is of pivotal importance:

> I cannot read between
> The lines of leaf and stone,
> For these are other eyes
> And the swift light has gone.
> By my birth-place the stream
> Rubs a wet flank, breaks free
> From the moored wall; escapes,
> Unwavering to sea.

What travel has done for Charles Causley as a writer has been to give him not only new situations but a means of leaving Cornwall: not to forget about it but to distance himself from the familiar things around him. It has given his poetry a new kind of freshness and an impetus which is still continuing. *21 Poems* (none of which appeared in periodicals) contains, perhaps significantly, proportionately more Cornish settings including 'Dick Lander', a shell-shocked victim of the Great War; 'Bridie Wiles', a local madwoman; and 'The Mystery of St, Mylor'. 'Gelibolu' (the Turkish name for Gallipoli) ends with a vision of the First World War; 'At The Chateâu Lake Louise' is a moving reflection on lost love; 'In The Dome-Car' is a metaphorical journey on a Canadian railway. There are also tributes to Edward Fitzgerald and the late W.S. Graham, three little pieces after the style of Emily Dickinson and a poem inspired by an Ashile Gorky picture. Causley at the age of 70 is still developing his art and looking for new ways of expression.

Looked at thematically however, *Secret Destinations* and all his more recent work are much more in continuity with his earlier poetry than might at first appear. And there is, I think, a growing unity about it, implied by the quotation from the Christian philosopher Martin Buber at the beginning of *Secret Destinations*: 'All journeys have secret destinations of which the traveller is unaware.' For whether Charles Causley is in the heart of Australia, the Canadian Rockies or in his own back yard, his journey is essentially one of self-discovery, an exploration of who he is and where he has come from. The result is neither self-regarding or confessional, but a body of poetry that, with craftsmanship, compassion and honesty continues to reflect the necessary condition of all human existence.

THE SCOP

(for Charles Causley)

Seamus Heaney

Every day in the hall, the struck harp,
The clear song of a skilled poet!
He told with mastery of man's beginnings
Long ago, how the Almighty had made the earth
A gleaming plain girdled with waters.
How in His splendour He set sun and moon
To be earth's lamplight, lanterns for men,
And filled the wide lap of the world
With branches and leaves. And how He quickened life
In every other moving thing as well.

(ll. 89–98 *Beowulf*)

A PARODY

Anthony Thwaite

I saw a thousand dashing grenadiers
Trooping the colour on the purple grass.
I thought when I had had a few more beers
I might make 'purple' 'red', but let that pass.

Their rifles sang like cuckoos in the night,
Their uniforms were bright as marzipan.
When in the mood, I can sit down and write
As jolly stuff as any jolly man.

This was published (over the pseudonym 'Herbert Blinco') in the *New Statesman* Weekend Competition, 30 June 1972. Competitors had been asked 'to compose poems in the manner of any living poet in running for the laureateship, celebrating any future event.' This was after C. Day Lewis's death and before the eventual appointment of John Betjeman. It was written with affection and admiration, as I think good parodies should be. It doesn't by any means say all I want to say about Charles Causley or his poetry, for whom I indeed have much affection and admiration. I hope it might amuse him, resurrected (the parody, I mean) after all these years.

Anthony Thwaite

TIMOTHY WINTERS

Charles Causley

Timothy Winters comes to school
With eyes as wide as a football pool,
Ears like bombs and teeth like splinters:
A blitz of a boy is Timothy Winters.

His belly is white, his neck is dark,
And his hair is an exclamation mark.
His clothes are enough to scare a crow
And through his britches the blue winds blow.

When teacher talks he won't hear a word
And he shoots down dead the arithmetic-bird,
He licks the patterns off his plate
And he's not even heard of the Welfare State.

Timothy Winters has bloody feet
And he lives in a house on Suez Street,
He sleeps in a sack on the kitchen floor
And they say there aren't boys like him any more.

Old Man Winters likes his beer
And his missus ran off with a bombardier,
Grandma sits in the grate with a gin
And Timothy's dosed with an aspirin.

The Welfare Worker lies awake
But the law's as tricky as a ten-foot snake,
So Timothy Winters drinks his cup
And slowly goes on growing up.

At Morning Prayers the Master helves
For children less fortunate than ourselves,
And the loudest response in the room is when
Timothy Winters roars 'Amen!'

So come one angel, come on ten:
Timothy Winters says 'Amen
Amen amen amen amen.'
Timothy Winters, Lord.
                    Amen.

Drawing by Ralph Steadman

EDEN ROCK

Charles Causley

They are waiting for me somewhere beyond Eden Rock:
My father, twenty-five, in the same suit
Of Genuine Irish Tweed, his terrier Jack
Still two years old and trembling at his feet.

My mother, twenty-three, in a sprigged dress
Drawn at the waist, ribbon in her straw hat,
Has spread the stiff white cloth over the grass.
Her hair, the colour of wheat, takes on the light.

She pours tea from a Thermos, the milk straight
From an old HP sauce-bottle, a screw
Of paper for a cork; slowly sets out
The same three plates, the tin cups painted blue.

The sky whitens as if lit by three suns.
My mother shades her eyes and looks my way
Over the drifted stream. My father spins
A stone along the water. Leisurely,

They beckon to me from the other bank.
I heard them call, 'See where the stream-path is!
Crossing is not as hard as you might think.'

I had not thought that it would be like this.

IN 1933

Charles Causley

I see the deep November street,
The crowd suddenly still beneath
The dark lurch of the Castle Keep
As though the evening held its breath
Before the bell-man's starting cry
And the first rocket hit the sky.

It was a children's land: a tower,
Ships, houses grumbling in low gear,
The stick-man stalking through the Square,
Paraffin torches slopping fire,
A child's heart too afraid to ask
Which was a face and which a mask.

I see the gold set-piece that read
'God Save Our Empire', as each head
In fireworks of the King and Queen
At the far end of Castle Green
Dribbled blue flame, began to sprout
Flowers of dark. Went slowly out.

BOULGE

Charles Causley

Edward FitzGerald sleeps
Under this sheet of stone,
Neat as never in life,
Innocent, alone.

The earth that he lies in is his.
Grass and willow-herb drown
The wilderness path through the trees.
The great house is down.

He longed to lie in birdsound.
To be ash. To dare
The salt of the ocean and find
Lodging there.

Flint-eyed, the church, the tower
Shadow his page.
Thinly the Persian rose
Frets in its cage.

It is He that hath made us. And he
Who is lying among
Hard voices of pebble and shard
Holds his tongue.

BRIDIE WILES

Charles Causley

Bridie Wiles, 2 Gas Court Lane,
Between the tanyard and the railway line,
About the time of the first Armistice
Scooped me, one Saturday, out of my pram.
Promised me the river.

My cousin Gwennie, nine,
And three foot eight to Bridie's five eleven
Said, 'You do
And I'll chuck you in too.
Anyway,
The water isn't deep enough today
To drown a frog in.'

'Nor is it,' Bridie said, sometimes
Quite sensible despite her role
As our local madwoman
Of Chaillot,
Making to bale me
Back into the pram,
If the wrong way round.

Decades on,
At Uncle Heber's Co-op funeral,
'I'll tell you something you don't know,'
Said Gwen.
'Between us, Bridie and me pulling
As if you were a Christmas cracker
We dropped you on your head.
I never told your mum. Or mine.
My God, but you went white!
We thought that you'd gone dead.

'Another thing.
It's always been a mystery to me
How you're the only one
Of our lot doing what you do.
The other day I read
That sort of thing can be set off
By a dint on the head.
Do you think that's true?
Perhaps you owe it all to Bridie and to me.'

I asked her what she meant by it and all.
'Not possible,' said cousin Gwen, 'to say.
Though Bridie may.'

Emerging from the Dome Car, Banff (Alberta) 1984

78

IN THE DOME-CAR

Charles Causley

The train, as if departure were a state-
Secret, pulls out without a sound. I glance
Up from *The Globe and Mail* surprised to see
Through the dome car's dull window, Canada
Lurching quietly by. *Find the dome car,*
You said to me. *You'll see it all from there.*

And so I do. Or think I do. At first,
The Bow River, surface of china blue,
Indigo-coloured water squeezing through;
The rail-cars straightening in line ahead.
Giacometti trees like naked men
Stand, sky-high, in a littleness of snow;
Adverts for Honda, holidays (*Try us
Ski Jasper*); hunks of rock; the red Dutch barn
Recurring like a decimal; a thin
Smear of gold-leaf that is the coming corn.

In ice-edged light the train moves cautiously
Above a toy village, a clip of black
And white Indian ponies, a tepee
Hoisted beside a brake of pointed sticks.
A bridge hurries to meet us; spills across
A frozen lake. A car parked on the ice,
In shifting light, glitters a mile from shore.
We gape at it. But what I see is you
Walking the long nave of the train-station,
Never turning. *You'll see it all from there.*

We rush the stone horizon. At the last
Moment the mountains part; admit us to
Indian country, where the patient snow
Refuses the year's passage, scars the floor
Of a pale valley; lies in wait for more.

Incident at freetown

Standing amongst the naked sailors
The smell of Africa blowing off
       shore
We lined up in front of the sick-bay
And banged on the young quacks'
      door.
  *
Stanny had been to see him before.
Come off shore with some extra loot:
Made the fatal mistake of loving
While not wearing on his sea-boot
  *
Chats when he fell down the
    hatch with a funny
Filled to the brim with boiling room
The lads caught the rum bucket of
    Conne,
Left old Chats to pull to Kingston
    Come.

80

Pongo Grew aley in Aleck,
Oxo merely his mother's heart,
Ivy -ever the sailors fancy -
Brought of shore from a Pompey
                    tart.
                *

The tiffy, I remember, looked more
                    like a doctor.
The quack himself looked nearer,
                    if at,
As though he was last man in
            for England,
The sky gone black & the
                    pitch gone red.
                *
Don't worry lads he said, as his
                    dipping the needle
Pumping it up with jungle juice.
No need Don't look. It's all over in a
                    second.
Not like putting your head in a noose.

We must all do our best for hygiene.
Don't forget to keep yourselves clean.
Chats & lice & nits & bedbugs
Save yourself for your wife, s. to me.

✳

We stuck out our arms. He stuck
in the needle.
We all for set to give out a roar.
The doctor swallowed his oath
to Hippocrates
And fell in a faint on the sick-bay
floor

✳

I looked at Chats & Chats looked at
me.
The Chief P.O. said Riff Jum. At the double. Oho.
One two!
Nobody got his injection for England.
The germs & the Germans broke
through

✳

The ship hit a mine in the
                    harbour at Craik
_____

The quack caught a shell at this
                    on the Norman patrol

The

Oxo & Porgo froze in the water
What may be said?

Oxo was lost in the a Northern patrol
_____

I went ashore with yellow fever
Twenty years later I saw Dr Hartley
Chromium-plated _____
.   Like a Charlie
Reminded him how he fell
                    down on the deck.

83

Lies, it's all lies, he said with

Why can't you get th^a way out of
                    your mind,
A dead man's a dead man
Put it behind you
        ——— Something put
                    behind.

_____

Some good men are killed by th
                    savage physician
Some by th statesman & some
            by th church,

Incident at Freetown

Lining up with the naked sailors
The smell of Africa blowing off-shore
I watched the sweat run down to
and   my ankles,
Borrowed a tickler from the man
                        next dow.

The sick-bay tiffy looked more like a
                        doctor.
The quack, ~~loned~~ nervous. His hand
                felt like lead,
As though he was last man in for
                England,
                turning
The sky ~~long~~ black + the pitch
                gone red.

85

Don't worry boys, he said; dipping the
                                        needle,

Pumping it full of jungle juice.
Don't look at the man in front, that's
                                the secret.
It's not ~~like~~ as if you're putting
                your head in a noose.

We stuck out our arms. He looked at
                his ~~the~~ needle.
We ~~all~~ ~~got~~ set for a run ashore.
~~But~~ the doctor swallowed his oath
~~and~~   to Hippocrates,
¡Fell in a faint through the sick-bay
                                door.

But nobody died of tropical disorders.
Nor one complained of feeling crook
~~The boys, it seemed, found f—day leaf~~
Malaria, dysentry, black-water
Pulled in their hmm till   fever
~~Held their fin~~   we pulled up the
                                    hook.

~~Through~~
~~But~~ Off the Greek island of Co,
                        a month later,
Where Hippocrates practised &
                lived his [ ] despair, & water.
Many died of ~~wounds, water, despair~~
                (including the doctor).
~~None of a form.~~ ~~But~~
(Including the doctor). ~~But~~ None of a form
                        Charles Causley

Many of my comrades died of wounds,
                        water, despair
(Including the doctor). None of a form.   cc

87

INCIDENT AT FREETOWN

Lining up ^on deck^ with the naked sailors,   11

The smell of Africa blown off-shore,   9

I watched the sweat run down to my
                           ankles,   10

Borrowed a tickler from the man next
                            door.   10

             *

The sick-bay tiffy looked more like a
    ^looked^   doctor,   11

The quack was nervous, his face of broad, 9

As though he was last man in for
                            10
with
                   England,

The sky gone black & the pitch
           ~~burned [turned~~ red. 9
    *   turned
              ? all   10

                                        as he   11
                                                          to
Don't worry, he said, I dipped the the needle
Pumped it full of the jungle-juice, 8
Don't look at the man in front,
              that's the secret.   11
It's not like putting your head in a
              noose.   Kump 10

                    *
              om
Hands on hips.
~~We stuck out our arms~~ He lorerd at
              his ~~the~~ needle   10
~~bishowing~~ the usual Naval   8
              restraint, his
Suddenly swallowed ~~the~~ oath to   12
              Hippocrates, ~~clas~~
Fell on the deck in a ~~number~~-one
                        number-one
              faint   10
                    *

89

I looked at Taff & Taff looked at
Chiefie 10

Liberty men, on shore! ~~Ate two~~
Nobody for a job ~~Fall in &~~
at Freetown his blood
~~whether your~~ blood was rum or gin.
10

*

No-me
~~Nobody~~ died of a tropical disorder
No-one complained of feeling crook
Malaria, ~~dysentery~~, blackwater-fever
~~Pulled in their horns till we~~ 12
lay down
low till we pulled our the
hook.
to

*

Black-water 9
fever

~~But~~
|Off the Greek islands, at Cos ~~a month~~ a month
out later ||
(Here Hippocrates lived (his Bum) 9
Most of them died of wounds or of 10
water,
Including the doctors ~~but none~~ None
of a germ. 10

Charles Causley

~~Whether~~

If his blood was of rum
rein ran
Whether his ~~blood~~ was of
rum or gin.

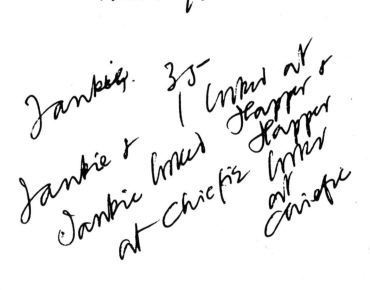

Janky
Oko   O xo 12

I looked at Jeff & Jeff looked at chiefs

Right turn!   Liberty men 8
                            fallin! 9

Nobody for a jab at freetown

Whether his veins ran
        rum or gin —— 8

Jankels.   35   I looked at
Jankie &   flapper
  Jankie looked   flapper
    at Chiefie   looked
                      at
                   chiefie

92

IMMUNITY

Charles Causley

Lining up with the naked sailors,
The smell of Africa blown offshore,
I watched the sweat run down to my ankles,
Borrowed a tickler from the man next door.

The sick-bay tiffy looked more like a doctor.
The quack was nervous, his face of bread;
He might have been last man in for England,
The sky gone dark and the pitch turned red.

'It's nothing,' he said as he dipped the needle,
Pumped it full of jungle juice.
'Don't look at the man in front, that's the secret.
It's not like putting your head through a noose.'

We stuck out our arms. He looked at his needle,
Showed the usual pusser's restraint,
Suddenly swallowed his oath to Hippocrates,
Fell on the deck in a number-one faint.

No one was issued with a jab at Freetown.
No one complained of feeling crook.
Malaria, yellow and blackwater fever
Lay down low till we pulled up the hook.

Rocked on the antiseptic ocean
Nobody noticed the turning screw.
'This could cost a fortune,' we said, 'in peace-time,
The sun so yellow and the sea so blue.'

And, for the record, off Kos a month later
Where Hippocrates lived out his term,
Most of them died of wounds or sea-water,
Including the doctor. None of a germ.

A KITCHEN IN THE MORNING

Charles Causley

I didn't know until I saw a copy of the first page of the *Daily Express* (price one halfpenny) for Friday, 24th August 1917, that I was born on the 1,117th day of the 'Great' War. The page makes sombre reading: not least, the report of a furious battle for a fortified slag-heap ('un-happy Huns among the ruins') at Lens, among the iron-foundries of Pas de Calais. Here, we read, the Canadians had some bayonet exercise, '. . . attacking and advancing with as great energy as when the battle began. The house and cellar fighting is entirely to their liking. They are wholly confident of their ascendancy over the enemy whenever he can be forced to fight man to man in the old fashioned way'.

I have no idea what my mother thought, if ever she read it, of such gruesome rubbish. My father was serving as a private soldier in France at the time; presumably her mind was on other things. Her maiden name was Bartlett ('little Bartholomew'), and I have always delighted at the marvellously unconscious prescience with which she produced me on St Bartholomew's Day. Unswervingly Church of England and lapped on all sides by the antiseptic tides of Cornish Methodism, I am fairly certain that she knew as little of the unfortunate flayed Saint's day as she did of the massacre of French Huguenots in 1572. At all events, I was named after my father, as he had been.

I have no memory of living in the house where I was born: the back cottage of a block of three in the lower part of the town. Past the front door ran the River Kensey (from the Cornish *kensa*: first and foremost), a swift, noisy flood that dashed its ten miles from Bodmin Moor to join the Devon boundary of the Tamar at the valley's end. The Kensey was a troublesome neighbour. In the heavy rains of autumn and winter, when the great granite sponge of the moor could hold no more, it turned a rich caramel colour, crossed the road and filled the cottages sometimes half-way up the stairs. There were thrilling tales of Grannie Bartlett's kitchen table, complete with her Singer sewing-machine in its wooden case, floating out of the front door and down-river towards the

Devon border. In summer, on the other hand, the Kensey sank and stank like a stranded whale.

The wall under the window of the room in which I was born was washed by Harper's Lake: the word 'lake' used here in the Cornish sense of 'stream'. Before the Reformation, the whole of the area had been a great Augustinian monastic foundation, and Harper's Lake was one of the ancient boundaries of the priory lands. Like all water-courses, it had its own, individual voice. Unlike the chattering Kensey, it ran darker and greener to a high, mosquito-like whine as it rushed beneath (sometimes through) the kitchen window and under the road to join up, unseen, with its larger neighbour. The sound of water counterpointed every activity in the cottages, and at night it was necessary to go down the slate-flagged communal 'passage' and out into the road to see if it was raining.

My mother, fearful of flood, was never at ease in the cottage. It bred in her a lifetime's fear of expanses of water: of lake and river and sea. But it was not this particular horror which drove her finally, while I was still an infant in arms, from the cottage. One evening, knitting by the light of the brass oil-lamp, she glanced up at the black, oak beams that ran across the kitchen ceiling. On one of the supports, where beam met wall, lay a rat calmly gazing down at her. That was enough. In my father's absence at the war, she was well-used to making decisions on her own. Within a month we had packed and moved to higher ground, a quarter of a mile away and half-way up the immensely steep hill to the town.

The house was part of a large, slate-hung tenement building. There were three dwellings at ground-level, separated from the hill by a low, brick wall just high enough to lean on comfortably. Perched above us were two flats, reached through a side-entrance and up an Italianate wooden staircase and along a landing. Also at the rear were a pair of communal lavatories and taps.

It was at this house that I spent almost the whole of my first ten years, and from which my first views of the life and work of my hometown were framed. The house was small: two bedrooms, a scullery or back-kitchen, and a living-room. The front-door opened directly, then, on a room that was a kitchen in the morning, but which after dinner at midday was transformed into a living-room by laying a thick, green velvet cloth hung with tassels over a table on which was also placed, dead-centre, a potplant. Though on the whole a depressingly 'good' boy, one of my earliest memories is of crawling under the table one afternoon and scissoring off all the tassels. As soon as my mother appeared, I was told later, I confessed: smiling with real pleasure. What Freud would have made of this I can't imagine.

From the living-room window, one saw the hill sloping dramatically—almost impossibly—across the pane. What was presented, unasked, to the viewer was a small stage-set peopled with characters pausing for breath on the way up, or walking—cautiously, and with short steps—down. Unbelievably mysterious sherds and shreds of conversation spilled and splintered in our direction. It was the scene of my first glimpses below the surface and into the unguessed-at secret lives of other people.

It is from this house, too, that I retrieve what fragmentary memories I have of my father. He was from the village of Trusham, in Devon. The Causleys had lived in Trusham for generations, though none lives there now. White's famous *Survey of Devon*, made in 1850, lists my great-grandfather Samuel Causley as the victualler of the New Inn (long since burned down), and his wife Sarah as the village school-mistress. She conducted her classes in a back-room of the pub. My father, working as a groom and gardener for a Teignmouth doctor, met my mother (exiled from Cornwall for a decade) while she was working as a domestic-servant in the Big House next door. They were married in Cornwall in 1915, and my mother lived with my widowed Grannie Bartlett in the cottage where I was born while my father was in France.

Such recollection as I have of him is small. My father is a tall, bony man, neatly dressed in tweeds and a cap, and with brightly-polished boots. He speaks with a cider-sharp, mid-Devon accent. He carries a stick or cane, and has a black-and-white terrier called Jack. Once, he took me to a race-meeting. All I remember are shouts, rain, the thump of hooves, of being able to see nothing in front of me but the backs of men's legs. He takes me to a travelling-fair and pays for me and my friend to ride on the swing-boats. I immediately feel sick and scream to be taken down. My friend is sad.

My father cannot tie a bootlace. The index-finger of his right hand is missing, following an accident while working with horses during a bombardment in France. Sometimes (like D. H. Lawrence, I learned years later) he is driven to furies of exasperation by uncontrollable fits of coughing.

What I did not know was that all the time I knew him, my father was a dying man. His service in France had shattered him physically. He was invalided out of the army in 1918 with a disability pension, and died in 1924 of pulmonary tuberculosis. Slowly, he seems to me to have withdrawn, or been withdrawn, from my consciousness. His presence receded, as it were, so delicately from me that I was hardly aware of his departure. In my mind is still a picture, on the night he died, of my mother and one of my aunts sitting by the glowing red grate of the black iron stove. It was late December, and I'd said I would go upstairs and see my father before I went to bed. For a second, my mother looked disconcerted; said something about him being 'with the angels now'. I became suddenly acutely aware that both my mother and my aunt were looking at me closely; that this was a significant moment, and that something was expected of me. My response must have disappointed them. 'Oh,' I said. The news made little impact. Then, it seemed almost a matter of indifference to me: though it was not to remain so all my life. But so it was that, firmly, my mother assumed officially the dual rôle she had in fact been forced to play for some time before my father's death: that of both parents.

I was, of course, already attending school. This was a huge, granite and slate Noah's Ark of a building beached, only five hundred yards away, on the sloping shores of the town allotments. It was a church school, built in 1840, and looked it. Most of the windows were high in the walls, some with little diamond-shaped panes framed in lead. The school bell was a sobering relic from a medieval chapel on the Castle Green, and had in its time tolled for executions when we were an Assize town. The lavatories, also antique, were a row of whitewashed booths flushed every ten minutes by a sudden bore, and roar, of water that very neatly moved all deposits a yard or so farther along the channel.

There were three 'elementary' schools in the town, and ours served one of the poorest districts: a steep triangle of cottages, alleys, lanes, courts and dead-ends between the red and grey stones of the Public Library and the town church. The most prominent building in this always lively, teeming area was the Lodging House, even taller than our tenement, and immediately

97

opposite the Gate Inn. The Lodging House (like the local Workhouse) occupied a position of terror in the mythology of the 'respectable' working-class that just, but often only just, clung on to solvency. It was a doss-house for what were called roadsters; sometimes the last stop before a permanency in the Workhouse. To me, its great doorway always menacingly open, the entrance seemed as wide and as easy to slip through as that to Hell. One could just catch a glimpse of a vast communal table, benches, a bare, slate-slabbed floor.

Up the road from the Lodging House lived my friend John French Treloar. John French, a tall, pale, gentle-voiced, gentle-mannered boy with a sweet singing voice, was named after the famous Field-Marshal. It was a sign of the times; other boys we knew were named for soldiers like Douglas Haig and Kitchener. John French sang in the town church choir, for which, he told me, boys got *paid*, with an extra shilling for weddings and funerals. His mother had died ten weeks after he was born, when, he once said, she had 'turned fifty'. We made, somehow, a good pair: and I appreciated, even at that age, his strength of character, his sense of humour. He spoke, with a delicate air of acceptance, and never complaint, of meals mostly of bread and jam; often of bread soaked in hot water with the addition of a lump of butter. Yet he contrived to radiate a feeling that, with luck, things might get better.

We sat together in the roaring elementary school, where we discovered, jointly, the world of English folk-song. The Head-master was 'Daddy' Nelson, a challenging, bachelor-figure second only to God. 'Daddy', permanently in a pepper-and-salt suit and with a Lancastrian pepper-and-salt voice to match, was an enthusiastic musician. On Friday afternoons, the squeaking glass screen dividing the two upper classrooms would be trundled back, and a black harmonium, bristling with stops, dragged into the centre of operations. Unquestionably in command, one gleaming boot placed diagonally across the two pedals, 'Daddy' Nelson stood at the harmonium (wise school-master, he never sat down) pumping breath into the instrument, his blazing eye sweeping like a beam from a lighthouse the ninety of us jammed in the inky oak and iron desks. So, we chanted our way through *Hymns Ancient and Modern, National Songs of the British Isles,* and—best of all—the volumes of English folk-songs collected by, among others, Cecil Sharp.

> Jackie boy. Master.
> Sing'ee well. Very well.
> Hey down. Ho down.
> Derry derry down,
> Among the leaves of the green O.

Were we aware—as James Reeves points out in *The Idiom of the People*—that 'the theme of sexual pursuit symbolized by a hunt is a commonplace in medieval poetry'? Certainly not; and my guess is that our teachers weren't aware of it either. But, almost unknown to me, the seeds of a love of poetry were planted.

Oddly, I remember little of what must have been read to us in the 'poetry' lessons. Apart from a fragment or two of strictly-abbreviated nursery-rhymes, there was the fact that Young Lochinvar came out of the west, and through all the wide Border his steed was the best. If anyone suggested just where in the west Young Lochinvar came out of, I don't recall it. As we were children in a Cornish school, I had a hazy notion that it might have been Penzance, or possibly Land's End. Then there were the lines of Tennyson:

> The splendour falls on castle walls
> And snowy summits old in story.

Louring above our classroom window was the ivy-strung and greenly disintegrating mass of a Norman castle, built on the earth-cone of an even earlier defence-work. I don't recollect a parallel being drawn between this fact and Tennyson's imaginative fiction. A mere four lines or so salvaged from seven years in an infant and junior school may suggest that the formal poetry lesson was not for me. At least, perhaps it was the beginning of an understanding that the precise disciplines of history and geography haven't much to do with the business of falling in love with a poem; that, rather, one listened to an individual voice, made an individual interpretation, constructed in the mind and imagination one's own entirely personal map and calendar.

It was at this time, too, in the 'silent' reading periods at school, that—conventionally enough, I suppose, for a bookish child—I came upon Stevenson's *Treasure Island, Don Quixote, David Copperfield*, all in abridged versions. To this day, I recall the fear I felt when I read of David, on the beach at Yarmouth, gallantly saying to Em'ly, 'You're quite a sailor, I suppose?'

> 'No,' replied Em'ly, shaking her head. 'I'm afraid of the sea'. 'Afraid?' I said, with a becoming air of boldness, and looking very big at the mighty ocean. '*I* an't!'
> 'Ah! but it's cruel,' said Em'ly. 'I have seen it very cruel to some of our men. I have seen it tear a boat as big as our house all to pieces.'

These words were to return to me, time and again, in 1940 when I found myself in a wartime destroyer in the Atlantic. But 'my' war, as it was to most of my generation, was over an unimaginable horizon in the 1920's.

We still lived in the long shadow of 1914–18. After my father's death, my mother set about supplementing her war-widow's pension by taking in washing. My maternal grandmother, Grannie Bartlett, had done precisely the same when her husband, a young quarryman, had been killed in a fall of slate in 1881, leaving her with seven young children. Once a week, we collected a wicker basket (to the Cornish, a 'flasket') of linen from one of the large local houses: trudging to and fro along Horse Lane, each clutching a handle. Drying the stuff, in an area perpetually needled by fine Atlantic rains, was a permanent problem; the back-kitchen seemed always hung with sheets. She also spent one day a week scrubbing and cleaning the house of a local shopkeeper, and on this day I went there from school for my midday meal. For her day's work, she received half-a-crown.

Her ability as a good 'manager', something on which great store was set among working-class women, was extraordinary. The house was always warm, clean, comfortable. There was plenty of food, and the weekly roast chicken was as regular as Sunday. She was always at home when I returned from school. She would have died rather than accept parish-relief or have dressed me in jumble-sale clothes or the cast-offs of other children. A cousin of mine, ten years older than me, got a job in the town and arrived as a lodger. And, amongst all else, she found a little time for reading from a two-penny library: novels by the Cornish writers Silas and Joseph Hocking (*Rosemary Carew*, by the latter, was a tremendous favourite) and *Stella Dallas* by the American Olive Higgins Prouty. She also had a few books of her own: *The Following of the Star* by Florence L. Barclay, *The Sorrows of Satan* by Marie Corelli, and the like. I tried them all, and enjoyed most: especially *Stella Dallas*, which exercised a peculiar fascination over me. I re-read it constantly and with such devotion that she grew apprehensive and forbade me ever to read it again. I couldn't think why; and not until years later did it occur to me that the central character was a prostitute. At all events, my mother forgot the ban, and nothing more was said about it.

There came the proud day when she decided that I should have piano-lessons. She bought a shiny, walnut-coloured second-hand instrument with brass candlesticks and what the dealer described inevitably as a 'lovely tone'. My music teacher came to the house on Tuesday afternoons. The green cloth was spread over the table, and she would sip a cup of tea and daintily eat a slice of my mother's homemade sponge-cake while I played scales or (after a couple of years) ripped my way through 'The Robin's Return'— the high point of my performance as a pianist in those days. I was also given a copy of a red-bound collection called *Songs that Won the War* and found myself, after a fashion, able to play them. Their words gripped me, especially in such grim parodies as, 'If you were the only Boche in the trench/And I had the only bomb'. There was another, even more fearful:

> 'If you want to find the old battalion,
> I know where they are . . .
> They're hanging on the old barbed wire'.

For the first time, I got a hint of the realities of life in the trenches, still largely unverbalized, experienced by the young men in the town who had returned from the war. By now, too, my father's name was inscribed (spelt wrongly, as it happened) on the war memorial of his native Devonshire village. 'Your father would have been proud of you,' my mother said when, rather to my surprise (I was always hopeless at arithmetic), I got a scholarship to the grammar school. Compliments from her, to my face, were rare. I was impressed.

By the end of this first decade of my life, the properties of the small Cornish town in which I lived had printed themselves indelibly on my imagination as an image of childhood. The town had been walled and fortified by the Normans, and to my mind they had never really left. The stone eye of the castle stared relentlessly down on every street and dyke. The huge jaws of its gateways gaped. To the east, over the northern rim of Dartmoor, was the escape-route to London; to the west, the ragged granite sea of Bodmin Moor. I often thought of the plight of those early soldiers of occupation. The whole ambience of Auden's 1937 poem 'Roman Wall Blues' became instantly part of my own imaginative territory when, ten years later, I first came upon it.

> Over the heather the wet wind blows,
> I've lice in my tunic and a cold in my nose.

The streets at night, in childhood, were darker; lit by gas, the lamp-lighter going every evening on his rounds. London, and the rest of the world, were unreachable, unattainable. We lived in a slate womb, and no-one ventured far. What enriched life for me was the torchlit, winter carnival, a genuine feast of fools, halfway between Michaelmas and Christmas; the silent films in the (originally) metal-roofed cinema run by a spry, ex-member of Fred Karno's famous troupe and who had performed with Chaplin and Stan Laurel; the exotic sight of an annual summer pilgrimage in honour of a 16th-century Roman Catholic seminary priest martyred in the town. At the little grammar school, there was a strangely disturbing shock of association with the last when I came across D. H. Lawrence's 'Giorno Dei Morti' in an anthology.

> Along the avenue of cypresses,
> All in their scarlet cloaks and surplices
> Of linen, go the chanting choristers,
> The priests in gold and black, the villagers . . .

Sharp-tongued, over-talkative, totally uninterested in any manifestation of sport, it was quickly borne in on me that I was never to be a 'popular' child. I was, alas, no longer the boy-wizard of the harmonium, accompanying 'Fierce raged the Tempest o'er the Deep' with great style at the morning assembly in the elementary school. One slight success came, however, when our

Welsh teacher of English began setting us poems to write for homework. My hitherto unguessed-at talent for writing verses suddenly came to the fore. It never made me popular, but the moment our teacher (notably chary of awarding high marks) gave me ten out of ten for a sonnet, I found myself regarded by my classmates with the healthy if limited respect accorded to—say—the double-jointed or the water-diviner. My poem, faintly anti-Semitic, was called 'The Jew'.

'Beneath yon towering palm-tree's lengthening shade,
Now as the brazen evening sun doth fade
A veritable Shylock of all Jews
Doth count his gold for fear that he might lose
One dinar of his hoarded, glittering pile,
While by him flows the muddy, sluggish Nile . . . '

I remember distinctly that I brought the Nile in because I couldn't think of anything more appropriate to rhyme with pile. We were also asked to write our own, personal versions of Rupert Brooke's 'The Great Lover'. All I recall of this is that something I loved was a musical-play I hadn't seen called *Lilac Time*, based on the life of Schubert. I was hypnotised by the sight and sound of certain words, and often got the meanings wrong. Inspired by the novels of the Baroness Orczy about the Scarlet Pimpernel, I wrote a piece about Robespierre.

O Robespierre, thou sea-green immobile,
Thy soul, deep-stained, was ice and did not feel . . .

There must have echoed, in my head, the celebrated description of Robespierre as the 'sea-green incorruptible'. Anyhow, I pronounced it 'immobeel'. In the days before radio taught listeners pronunciation, one did one's best with 'hard' words. For years, I never associated 'appendicitis' ('appen-dickitus') with a complaint called 'pendy-situs'. To this day, I have to restrain myself from calling Nicaragua 'Nickera-gooa'. Once, in the elementary school, we were asked to name a steep, local footpath. My hand was the first to be raised. 'The Adjackant Rocks'. The class howled with laughter; everyone knew the local name, 'Zig Zag'. But wasn't there a painted sign at the entrance: 'Pedestrians are Warned that Stones occasionally Fall from the Adjacent

Rocks'? Ever unadept at defending myself, I said nothing.

One day we were set an essay on what we would like to be when we left school. I had no idea, and consulted my mother. 'Put down "solicitor's clerk",' she said. 'That's a good job'. So, rightly certain of my own intellectual limitations, I did. And I comforted myself with the thought that maybe Education with a capital 'e' was not for me. Later in my teens, on a first visit to London, I bought for one-and-six in the Charing Cross Road, a red-covered copy of *The War Poems of Siegfried Sassoon*. It was my first clear view of my father's world of 1914–18, and I went on to read Graves, Blunden, Owen. I had by this time also struck up a friendship with a young, unemployed linotype-operator, six or seven years older than myself. He lived in a street at the back of the Lodging House, was a member of the Left Book Club, and lent me (among much else) his copy of Orwell's *The Road to Wigan Pier*. Somehow, too, I came upon the poems of Auden, Spender, Day-Lewis, MacNeice; Isherwood's *Goodbye to Berlin*.

But all this was ahead of the July day, in my sixteenth year, when I had just finished sitting the School Certificate examination. I came home from school, and to my amazement my mother said, 'I've got you a job with Mr Finn the builder. In the office. Start after next week. Wages, twelve-and-six'. I don't know if I showed it, but it was the greatest shock of my life. It didn't occur to me to protest. All I knew was that I was trapped, absolutely without qualifications of any kind. It was the end of the world.

By St. Thomas Water

SO SLOWLY TO HARBOUR

Charles Causley

Apart from the war years, and my years as a student, I lived the whole of my life, up to 1971, at home and in my mother's house. I was teaching then in the school where I had once been a pupil myself. In the evenings, after my school work was done, I read; wrote my poems—slowly, arduously, then as now. During the preceding years in the navy, the world had gradually opened up to me: a young Cornishman who had never as much as crossed the Channel to France. In war, I ranged about from West Africa to Sydney, from Scapa Flow to New Guinea and the islands of the Pacific. After 1947, from Dublin to Warsaw and Moscow; from East and West Berlin to Naples; and, many times, to Spain. But always, when the autumn school-bell rang, I returned home to Cornwall to teach, to eat my mother's cooking, to write.

The thought of what my reaction would be to my mother's death often troubled me—even more so, the thought of what I should do if she became an invalid, immobile, incapable of looking after herself. What kind of a person was my mother, and what was the well-spring of her nature? I think there is an important clue to be found in something that happened one winter evening at home, in the late 1950s.

I had been writing, but had stopped to watch a Greek play on television. A group of desolate women, many clutching children, stood lamenting loudly in a rock landscape of destruction and death. The door of my room opened, and my mother appeared with some coffee. She took in the scene on the screen at a glance. 'What,' she said, a little coolly, I thought, 'is the matter with them?' 'There has just been a great war, mother,' I said. 'They have lost husbands, lovers, homes, hope for the future. They are bewailing their fate.' My mother looked extremely unsympathetic. 'Why,' she said decisively, 'don't they go out to work? Like I did.' Exit. I switched off the set. There seemed little point in watching the rest; more in pondering what she had said.

My mother was a woman totally unused to relying on others. In everything but the moral sense—a very important exception, I recognised then, as now—she relied very little on me. I pushed thoughts of her future, and mine, from my head. No sense in worrying: it might never happen. Except that, in 1966, it did, when a stroke robbed her of all except speech and the ability to feed herself with one hand—her left hand. Just what a blessing the retention of at least these two functions was, I quickly grew to appreciate in the years that followed.

In a matter of seconds, she had crossed that invisible, but terrifyingly real frontier, that divides the sick from the well. And, unwillingly, I crossed that frontier in her wake.

At the outset, I found it extremely difficult to recognise the situation for exactly what it was. To define it clearly, I thought, would magnify its difficulties; but I was wrong. In writing to my friends about what had happened, for example, I could not, at first, bring myself to use the word 'stroke'. For years at home, I suppose, it had been a word of fear; one unconsciously taboo. But when I did manage to get it down in writing, it seemed to diminish the bogey slightly; though not, I remember thinking grimly, for the patient.

It was clear that she would need full-time nursing and care. People, as ever, were full of advice. The best came from Oscar Wilde: 'All advice is bad, and good advice is absolutely fatal.' The general opinion was that, as a bachelor with neither brothers nor sisters, I should put my mother in a long-term geriatric hospital; that I should on no account give up my teaching and stay at home and look after her. I got the impression that, had I been a woman, especially a single woman, I should have been expected—totally unfairly, as I see it—quite automatically to have done the exact opposite.

To this day, I do not know what I should have done if an old schoolfriend, at a moment of terrible crisis and desperation for me, had not come forward and said quietly: 'Don't worry; I will look after your mother while you are at school.' If ever a saint—I shall call her B—stood before me, it was then. She was experienced in geriatric nursing. For nearly five years, she came to the house five-and-a-half days a week; cooked, washed, cleaned; saw to my mother's needs; fed the cats; remained resolutely cheerful and absolutely imperturbable and tactful in the face of the battalions of major and minor disasters that accompany crippling illness and old age. And she bustled off to re-enter the world of her own family and her ex-merchant-seaman husband each day at four o'clock, when I got home from school.

The arrival of B decided me. I would keep my mother at home. It was a hazardous prospect. She might die in an hour; or in ten years. If I was to be the survivor of the pair of us, I could see no alternative after my mother's death, to a period of illness, breakdown, myself. This seemed to be the pattern of such cases. But I also knew that I must try to avoid or minimise any reason for remorse or personal guilt at having failed or abandoned my mother in an hour of crisis. This, at the end of the story, would for me have rendered personal grief totally unbearable. And so the family roles were reversed. My mother was now the child. I became her parent—both parents. Though they had both died before I was born, I came to know them—slowly, curiously— better than I ever had before.

Life resolved itself into an iron pattern. From four in the afternoon till school-time the next morning, I was alone with my mother; and for most of the weekend. The pressures of organising a day or two away from home, or, once, a week's holiday, were so great that, in the end, I found it much less of a strain not to go at all.

Did I feel like a jailer, serving a sentence alongside the prisoner? Not really. The choice of life was mine; I could have changed it easily. Too easily. But what kept me going?

One supreme advantage I had over those who care for the elderly sick for 24 hours a day was that I was at school in the disarming company of young children, for seven hours of the 24. The young, very properly, are absorbed in their own problems. And, unknowingly, they were able to absorb me in them, too; able to give some kind of balance and proportion, when I emerged at the end of the afternoon, to mine. Physically, combined with my stint of home nursing, it was all tremendously punishing; but it helped my survival. I saw in those children the promise of tomorrow; something, I hope, my mother also saw in the faithful daily visits of a young mother and her newly-born baby from next door.

And there were a thousand other contributory factors to survival. There was the example of my mother's marvellous patience. There she would sit, quite unable to stir, one or other of the cats on her lap. All day, she would watch the seasons slowly alter the colours of the tall hedgerow beyond the living-room window.

After the evening meal, I would sit and write for an hour. This was absolutely vital to me. I was at no time prevented by circumstances from getting words down on paper. Of all the arts—mercifully for me, then—the material demands of writing poetry are the smallest. A pencil, a notebook; long, quiet hours in which to turn over thoughts—these were enough.

And I talked to my mother a lot about her childhood, her long past. She had been approaching 80 when she first fell ill. And through the simple, clear glass she held up, I found myself able to observe as if with new eyes, my own childhood; and I wrote about it in poem after poem. Of the rather sinister and now disused quarry, below a steep cliff path called Zig Zag, where her own father, as a young quarryman, had been killed in a fall of slate. Of a travelling dancing-bear, made to perform for the children at her school in the 1890s. Her natural sympathy for the bear seemed to me as sensitive and as sharp as when she had first observed it. Of the house where I was born: 'Riverside', by the gas-works; and of how the mothers would bring their young babies and hold them over the wall, believing the smell of coal-gas to be a certain remedy for whooping-cough. And my mythical Uncle Stanley, after whom I was named: her youngest, dearest brother who emigrated before 1914 and died while serving in the Canadian army. I remember the tears she shed on his birthday— over 60 years after she had last seen him. The family past, the tribal memories, long dark, suddenly glowed; burst into flame.

Her simple, Christian faith never wavered. She never sought, consciously, to impose it on others; certainly not, since the statutory days of Sunday School, on me. I lost my faith in the Thirties; but, 20 years later, achieved the beginnings of a kind of recovery. At heart, I knew that her faith was the same as mine. A forest, a church, an art gallery, a seascape, a concert-hall, a river valley, a theatre, an expanse of moorland, all these were in one important respect the same to us both: temples of the spirit in which life, and its creator, were to be reverenced. She loved a church service, and for 75 years had hardly missed one of a Sunday. On the other hand, my feeling was—still is—that of Emerson: 'I like the silent church before the service begins better than any preaching.'

She preferred *Hymns Ancient and Modern* to my *Oxford Book of English Verse*. I liked them both. Her knowledge of the words of those hymns was prodigious, and her memory of the poems of her Victorian schooldays more than once put me to shame. William Howitt's 'The Wind in a Frolic', for instance.

> The wind one morning sprung up from sleep,
> Saying, 'Now for a frolic! now for a leap!
> Now for a mad-cap, galloping chase!
> I'll make a commotion in every place!

These simple and profound consolations of religion and of art were very great. For me, there was no dividing-line between the two. But it would be foolish to deny that—constantly, desperately—I had to remind myself that what was happening to us both was not unending; that it was a dark season, illuminated by unexpected bursts of light. Of course, there were periods of terrible tension. My mother's only cure—and it was painful to acknowledge it—was death. It was impossible, sometimes, to avoid the feeling that one was being tugged into the same grave. Death, monumentally, took its time as the body—and I wrote this in a poem—slid 'slowly, O so slowly, to harbour'. Most frightening of all was the realisation that one was in the classic situation—should hope have been utterly lost—of one who, in awful despair, kills first the patient and then himself.

But to recognise the fact that despair was the greatest evil, the greatest enemy, was also to begin its conquest. I felt like a man tossed on a bleak sea, who must not lose sight of the light on the shore. In the last stages of my mother's illness, I felt, helplessly, both spectator of, and participant in, a drama as old as the world itself. My good friend B herself fell ill, and could help me no longer. My mother grew worse; an assortment of illnesses placed her beyond the limits of care at home. By the time, finally, inevitably, she reached the geriatric hospital, a kind of curtain had already descended between her and the rest of the world. As always, through her long passage of illness, I found it difficult to acknowledge changes of character, of nature; it was hard to recognise, clearly and dispassionately, that the person I once knew was now someone else; that things could never be the same again. I was conscious, too, that she was paying the price of my own freedom. And the price was that of dying in public.

I was assailed by two fears. Would her death, when it came, be with dignity? Would I be there? I was obsessed by the thought that, after having spent so many years at her side, I should leave her to die alone after all. But those saintly nurses and orderlies in that geriatric ward saw to it that this was not so.

After her death, on a cold, quiet, sunny November afternoon, I had no difficulty whatever in choosing her epitaph: 'Blessed are the pure in heart: for they shall see God.'

The following summer, I was in Israel, in the Sanctuary Church of the Beatitudes, among the hills where Christ had preached the Sermon on the Mount. There the words were again: 'Blessed are the pure in heart: for they *shall* see God.' Through the great window, I could see the Lake of Galilee: burning blue as the water in my mother's old, galvanised-iron washtub, after she had put in the blue-bag on a childhood Monday in Cornwall, half a century before.

This article was first broadcast as one of a series of Lent talks on BBC Radio 4, 1977)

With Ted Hughes and Seamus Heaney, Arvon Foundation 1980. (Photo by Carol Hughes)

Stephen McIntyre as Billy Bedlam, Ruth Borman as Alice ('The Doctor & The Devils'. The Banff Centre, Alberta, 1984)

CHARLES CAUSLEY: A SELECT BIBLIOGRAPHY

Barry Newport

Selections and Collections:

PENGUIN MODERN POETS 3 (with George Barker and Martin Bell: Penguin, 1962).
CHARLES CAUSLEY AND KATHLEEN RAINE (Harlow: Longman, 1969).
CHARLES CAUSLEY AND LAURIE LEE (Oxford: Pergamon Press, 1970).
COLLECTED POEMS 1951–1975 (Macmillan, 1975; Boston: Godine, 1975).

Separate Works:

RUNAWAY (Curwen, 1936). *Play*
THE CONQUERING HERO (Curwen, 1937; New York: Schirmer, 1937). *Play*
BENEDICT (Muller, 1938). *Play*
HOW PLEASANT TO KNOW MRS LEAR. (Muller, 1948). *Play*
FARWELL, AGGIE WESTON (Aldington, Kent: Hand and Flower Press, 1951).
Poems
HANDS TO DANCE (Carroll and Nicholson, 1951). *Short Stories*—Republished as
Hands to Dance and Skylark (Robson, 1979); contains a Foreword and a 27 page
autobiographical Afterword.
SURVIVOR'S LEAVE (Aldington, Kent: Hand and Flower Press, 1953). *Poems*
UNION STREET (Hart-Davis, 1957; Boston: Houghton Mifflin, 1958). *Poems*
THE BALLAD OF CHARLOTTE DYMOND (Dartington, Devon, 1958). *Poem*—
Privately printed.
JOHNNY ALLELUIA (Hart-Davis, 1961). *Poems*
BALLAD OF THE BREAD MAN (Macmillan, 1968). *Broadsheet Poem*—Issued as a
'flier' for *Underneath The Water.*
UNDERNEATH THE WATER (Macmillan, 1968). *Poems*
JOHNNY ALLELUIA (Crediton, Devon: Richard Gilbertson, 1968). *Poem*—Limited
edition.
FIGURE OF 8 (Macmillan, 1969). *Poems*
I SAW A JOLLY HUNTER (Stoke Ferry, Norfolk: Daedalus Press, 1970). *Poetry Card*
FOR A BOOK OF CHILDREN'S VERSE (Stoke Ferry, Norfolk, 1970). *Poetry Card*
FIGGIE HOBBIN (Macmillan, 1970; actually Feb. 1971; New York: Walker, 1973).
Poems
INNOCENT'S SONG (Exeter, Devon: Exeter College of Art, 1971). *Poster Poem*
ZELAH (Evans Bros., 1972). *Broadsheet Poem*—Issued as an insert in *Child Education
Quarterly.*
THE TAIL OF THE TRINOSAUR (Leicester: Brockhampton Press, 1972; actually
March 1973). *Story in Verse*
SIX WOMEN (Richmond: Keepsake Press, 1973). *Poem*—Limited edition.
INFANT SONG (Arts Council of Great Britain, 1974). *Poetry Card*

WARD 15 (Words Press, 1974). *Poem*—Limited edition.
AS I WENT DOWN ZIG ZAG (Warne, 1974). *Poem*
THE HILL OF THE FAIRY CALF (Hodder & Stoughton, 1976). *Story in Verse*
HERE WE GO ROUND THE ROUND HOUSE (Leicester: New Broom Press, 1976). *Poem*—Limited edition.
DICK WHITTINGTON (Puffin, 1976). *Story*
THE GIFT OF A LAMB (Robson, 1978). *Verse-Play*
THREE HEADS MADE OF GOLD (Robson, 1978). *Story*
THE LAST KING OF CORNWALL (Hodder & Stoughton, 1978). *Story*
THE ANIMALS' CAROL (Macmillan, 1978). *Poem*
THE BALLAD OF AUCASSIN AND NICOLETTE (Kestrel, 1981). *Play*
NEW YEAR'S EVE, ATHENS (Ashington, Northumberland: Midnag, 1979). —Poetry Poster No. 49.
HYMN (North Tawton, Devon: Morrigu Press, 1983). —Limited edition.
SECRET DESTINATIONS (Macmillan, 1984)
AT CANDLEMAS (North Shields, Tyne and Wear: Iron Press, 1984). —Limited edition Poetry Poster.
VERSES FOR A FIRST NIGHT (Banff, Alberta, Canada: Banff Centre, 1984). —Broadsheet produced for the first performance in Canada of Causley's adaptation of Dylan Thomas's *The Doctor and the Devils* (unpublished).
TWENTY-ONE POEMS (Shipston-on-Stour, Warwickshire: Celandine Press, 1986). —Limited edition.
QUACK! SAID THE BILLY-GOAT (Walker Books, 1986; New York: Harper, 1986. *Poem*
EARLY IN THE MORNING (Viking Kestrel, 1986). *Poems*

Translations:

SLEEPER IN A VALLEY (St. Saviour, Jersey: Robert Tilling, 1979. —From the French of Arthur Rimbaud. Limited edition broadsheet.
TWENTY-FIVE POEMS BY HAMDIJA DEMIROVÍC (Richmond: Keepsake Press, 1980). —Limited edition.
SCHONDILIE (Leicester: New Brom Press, 1982). —Anonymous German ballad. Limited edition.
KING'S CHILDREN (Ashington, Northumberland: MidNAG, 1986). —German ballads.

Edited by Charles Causley:

Most of the following also contain introductions:
PENINSULA (Macdonald, 1957).
DAWN AND DUSK (Leicester: Brockhampton Press, 1962; New York: Watts, 1963).
RISING EARLY (Leicester: Brockhampton Press; New York: Watts, 1965).
MODERN FOLK BALLADS (Studio Vista, 1966).
SELECTED POEMS OF FRANCES BELLERBY (Enitharmon Press, 1970). —Limited edition.

IN THE MUSIC I HEAR (Gillingham: ARC, 1970).
—Poems by pupils of Launceston Voluntary Primary School.
OATS AND BEANS AND BARLEY: more poems from pupils of Launceston Primary School (Gillingham: ARC, 1971).
THE PUFFIN BOOK OF MAGIC VERSE (Puffin, 1974).
THE PUFFIN BOOK OF SALT-SEA VERSE (Puffin, 1978).
THE BATSFORD BOOK OF STORIES IN VERSE FOR CHILDREN (Batsford, 1979).
THE SUN, DANCING (Kestrel, 1982).

Uncollected prose contributions to books and periodicals (excluding reviews):

'Man into Fox'. *The Adelphi* (July–September 1949) 279–282.
—Essay on Henry Williamson.
Letter to the editor. *The London Magazine* (April 1956) 65–66.
'Gateway to Cornwall'. *The Listener* (3 January 1957) 10.
'Cornwall's White Witches'. *The Listener* (3 July 1958) 10.
'The World of Jack Clemo'. *The London Magazine* (October 1960) 41–44.
Introduction to THE MAP OF CLAY by Jack Clemo (Methuen, 1961).
'April Memories'. *The Listener* (13 April 1961) 646.
'My First Winter'. *The Listener* (21 December 1961) 1063–1064.
Response to Questionnaire. *The London Magazine (New Series)* (February 1962) 40–41.
POET'S CHOICE, edited by Paul Engle and Joseph Langland (New York: The Dial Press, 1962)
Contains a statement by Charles Causley, explaining his reasons for choosing 'A Visit to Van Gogh', pp. 159–160.
'A Poet Looks at Cornwall'. *The Listener* (4 July 1963) 7–8.
'The Stone Man'. *The Listener* (2 January 1964) 15–16.
—Essay on the Cornish sculptor Nevill Northey Burnard.
Autobiographical statement, pp. 158–159, in THE POETRY OF WAR, edited by Ian Hamilton (Alan Ross, 1965).
Statement about his poetry, pp. 17–18, in POETS OF OUR TIME, edited by F.E.S. Finn (Murray, 1965).
MASTER POEMS OF THE ENGLISH LANGUAGE, edited by Oscar Williams (New York: Dial Press, 1966).
—Contains an essay, pp. 998–1001, about Wilfred Owen, with particular reference to his poem 'Greater Love'.
Introduction to AN OCTAVE: poems by Siegfried Sassoon published in honour of his eightieth birthday (Privately printed, 1966).
'Charles Causley writes…' Poetry Book Society Bulletin (Spring 1968) 1–2.
'Tribute to Erica Marx'. *P.E.N. Newsletter* (Spring 1970) 4–5.
—Erica Marx, proprietor of the Hand and Flower Press, was Charles Causley's first poetry publisher.
CONTEMPORARY POETS OF THE ENGLISH LANGUAGE, edited by Rosalie Murphy (St. James Press, 1970).
—Contains an essay, pp. 202–203, about Jack Clemo.

115

Preface to AN ANTHOLOGY OF POEMS: SALTASH JUNIOR SCHOOL (Saltash, Cornwall, 1973).

'A Precise Reticence'. *The London Magazine N.S.* (December 1973–January 1974) 16–20.

—Article about William Plomer, reprinted in POETRY DIMENSION 2 (Robson, 1974).

LET THE POET CHOSE, edited by James Gibson (Harrap, 1973).

—Contains a statement, pp. 46, about his choice of 'Prinz Eugen' and 'A Short Life of Nevill Northey Burnard'.

Introduction to RICHARD HOOKER AND COMPANY (Exeter: Dept. of English, Exeter University, 1973).

Autobiographical essay, pp. 18–23 in WORLDS, edited by Geoffrey Summerfield (Penguin, 1974).

Obituary tribute to Frances Bellerby. *The Times* (7 August 1975) 14.

'Bands of Hope and Glory'. *The Sunday Times* (12 October 1975) 35.

—Article on Brass Bands.

'ABC', an autobiographical essay, pp. 5–16, in BOTH SIDES OF TAMAR, edited by Michael Williams (Bodmin, Cornwall: Bossiney Books, 1975).

Preface to POEMS FOR THE PARSON (Morwenstow, Cornwall: St. Mark's School, 1975).

—Poems by pupils to mark the Hawker Centenary.

Foreword to THE BOOK OF LAUNCESTON, by Arthur Bate Venning (Chesham, Bucks: Barracuda Books, 1976).

'A Modern Prelude'. *Books and Bookmen* (March 1977) 34–35.

—Article about Sir John Betjeman.

'So Slowly to Harbour'. *The Listener* (17 March 1977) 337–338.

—Autobiographical essay, with particular reference to his mther's last illness.

'In The Angle of the Waters'. *The Listener* (22 September 1977) 368–370.

—Autobiographical essay.

TWENTIETH CENTURY CHILDREN'S WRITERS, edited by D.L. Kirkpatrick (Macmillan, 1978).

—Contains essays on Kevin Crossley-Holland, p. 326; Ted Hughes, pp. 630–631; and Brian Patten, pp. 979–980.

'Launceston'. *The Observer Colour Magazine* (1 July 1979) 45–47.

—Reprinted in VILLAGE ENGLAND, ed. by Peter Crookston (Hutchinson, 1980).

Foreword to THOSE FIRST AFFECTIONS, edited by Timothy Rogers (Routledge & Kegan Paul, 1979).

Introduction to A BOOK OF THE WEST by S. Baring-Gould (Wildwood House, 1981).

'A Kitchen in the Morning'. *The Poetry Review* (June 1982) 33–38.

'Some Thoughts on Poetry and the Child'. *Education* (Wellington, N.Z., vol. 31 no. 1—no date) 31–34.

—Reprinted in WORD MAGIC, edited by Walter McVitty (New Zealand, Primary English Teaching Association, 1985).

Introduction to THE SPLENDID SPUR by Sir Arthur Quiller-Couch (Anthony Mott, 1983).

'Charles Causley writes . . .'. *Poetry Book Society Bulletin* (Autumn 1984) 2.

Introduction to POETRY PLEASE! (Dent, 1985).

Foreword to WESTERN MORNING VIEWS, compiled by Crispin Gill and James Mildren (Dartmouth, Devon: Harbour Books, 1985).
'My First Book'. *The Author* (Autumn 1985) 65–66.

Interviews;

Williams, Michael. Charles Causley. *The Cornish Magazine* (May 1963) 20–21.
Pett, John. Of Tigers and Trees. *The Guardian* (15 January 1965) 13.
Hidden, Norman. Haiku in the Park. *The Times Educational Supplement* (17 November 1972) 21.
Gardner, Raymond. In *The Guardian* (27 August 1975) 8.
Burton, Richard. The Monster Success of the Trinosaur. *The Cornwall Courier* (15 July 1976) 9.
Gregory, Colin. Scanning his Life. *The Western Morning News* (20 January 1978) 4.

Selected writings about Charles Causley in books and periodicals:

Currey, R.N. In *Poets of the 1939–1945 War* (Writers and their Work, no. 127), pp. 30–32. Longman, 1960.
Jennings, Elizabeth. In *Poetry Today, 1957–1960* (Supplement to British Book News), pp. 38–39. Longman, 1960.
Parker, Derek. Charles Causley. *The Cornish Review (new Series)* no. 3 (Autumn 1966) 18–22.
Kosok, Heinz. To a Poet Who has Never Travelled. In Oppel, H. (ed.), *Die moderne englische Lyrik*, pp. 276–286. Erich Schmidt Verlag, 1967.
Hidden, Norman. Teacher-Poets 1. *The Teacher* (14 July 1972) 8.
Thwaite, Anthony. In *Poetry Today 1960–1973* (Supplement to British Book News), pp. 32–33. Longman 1973.
Chambers, Aidan. Charles Causley and *The Tail of the Trinosaur*. *The Horn Book* (Boston, USA) (August 1975) 406–410.
Parker, Derek. A Poet's Progress. *The Western Morning News* (22 August 1975) 8.
McInnes, Colin. Progession: Schoolteacher/Vocation: Poet. *The Times Educational Supplement* (19 September, 1975) 26.
Scannell, Vernon. In *Not Without Glory*, pp. 126–133. The Woburn Press 1976.
Magee, Wes. Poetry Hits. *Teacher's World* (2 April, 1976) S.3.
Deadman, Ron. The Craft of Causley. *Teacher's World* (15 October 1976) S.11.
Cook, Stanley. Modern authors 11: Charles Causley. *The School Librarian* (December 1976) 304–308.
Levy, Edward. The Poetry of Charles Causley. *P.N. Review 6* (n.d., 1977) 46–48.
Parini, Jay. Tradition and Experiment: Charles Causley and Christopher Middleton. *The Chicago Review* (Summer 1977) 134–144.
Neale, John. The Magic of Words. *Cornish Life* (September 1977) 14–15.
Bell, Anthea. In *Twentieth Century Children's Writers*, pp 234–235. Macmillan, 1978.
Schmidt, Michael. In *50 Modern British Poets*, pp. 291–296. Pan 1979.
Tamplin, Ronald. As New as it is Old. *New Poetry* no. 45 (n.d., 1979) 4–9

Chambers, Aidan. Something Rich and Strange. *The Horn Book* (February 1979) 111–115

McVitty, Walter. Poetry—with lots of spaces for the children. *The Age* (Melbourne, Australia) (3 May 1980) 26.

Chambers, Aidan. In *Plays considered as Literature as well as Theatre for Young People from the ages of 8–18*, pp. 39–40 and pp. 49–51. The Thimble Press, Stroud, 1982.

Philip, Neil. Magic in the Poetry of Charles Causley. *Signal* (September 1982) 139–151.

Gioia, Dana. In *Poets of Great Britain and Ireland 1945–1960* (Dictionary of Literary Biography, vol. 27), pp. 40–49. Gale Research Co., Detroit, 1984.

Thwaite, Anthony. In *Contemporary Poets* (4th edition), pp. 127–129. St. James's Press, 1985.